The Trial of Adolf Eichmann

The Holocaust on Trial

FAMOUS
TRIALS

Titles in the Famous Trials series include:

The Trial of Adolf Eichmann

The Holocaust on Trial

by Bruce L. Brager

FAMOUS
TRIALS

Lucent Books, San Diego, CA

Library of Congress Cataloging-in-Publication Data

Brager, Bruce L., 1949–
  The trial of Adolf Eichmann / by Bruce L. Brager.
    p. cm. — (Famous trials.)
  Includes bibliographical references and index.
  Summary: Chronicles the trial of the Nazi war criminal, which became a reminder to the world of the horrors of the Jewish Holocaust.
  ISBN 1-56006-469-2 (lib. : alk. paper)
  1.Eichmann, Adolf, 1906–1962—Trials, litigation, etc.—Juvenile literature. 2. War crime trials—Jerusalem—Juvenile literature. 3. Holocaust, Jewish (1939–1945)—Juvenile literature. [1. Eichmann, Adolf, 1906–1962—Trials, litigation, etc. 2. War crime trials. 3. Holocaust, Jewish (1939–1945)]
  I. Title. II. Series.
KMK44.E33B73   1999
364.15'1'092—dc21   98-30258
                                                          CIP
                                                          AC

Copyright © 1999 by Lucent Books, Inc.
P.O. Box 289011
San Diego, CA 92198-9011
Printed in the U.S.A.

18.95

Table of Contents

Foreword

"The law is not an end in and of itself, nor does it provide ends. It is preeminently a means to serve what we think is right."

William J. Brennan Jr.

THE CONCEPT OF JUSTICE AND THE RULE OF LAW are hallmarks of Western civilization, manifested perhaps most visibly in widely famous and dramatic court trials. These trials include such important and memorable personages as the ancient Greek philosopher Socrates, who was accused and convicted of corrupting the minds of his society's youth in 399 B.C.; the French maiden and military leader Joan of Arc, accused and convicted of heresy against the church in 1431; to former football star O.J. Simpson, acquitted of double murder in 1995. These and other well-known and controversial trials constitute the most public, and therefore most familiar, demonstrations of a Western legal tradition that dates back through the ages. Although no one is certain when the first law code appeared or when the first formal court trials were held, Babylonian ruler Hammurabi introduced the first known law code in about 1760 B.C. It remains unclear how this code was administered, and no records of specific trials have survived. What is clear, however, is that humans have always sought to govern behavior and define actions in terms of law.

Almost all societies have made laws and prosecuted people for going against those laws, but the question of which behaviors to sanction and which to censure has always been controversial and remains in flux. Some, such as Roman orator and legislator Cicero, argue that laws are simply applications of universal standards. Cicero believed that humanity would agree on what constituted illegal behavior and that human laws were a mere extension of natural laws. "True law is right reason in agreement with nature," he wrote,

6

world-wide in scope, unchanging, everlasting. . . . We may not oppose or alter that law, we cannot abolish it, we cannot be freed from its obligations by any legislature. . . .This [natural] law does not differ for Rome and for Athens, for the present and for the future. . . . It is and will be valid for all nations and all times.

Cicero's rather optimistic view has been contradicted throughout history, however. For every law made to preserve harmony and set universal standards of behavior, another has been born of fear, prejudice, greed, desire for power, and a host of other motives. History is replete with individuals defying and fighting to change such laws—and even to topple governments that dictate such laws. Abolitionists fought against slavery, civil rights leaders fought for equal rights, millions throughout the world have fought for independence—these constitute a minimum of reasons for which people have sought to overturn laws that they believed to be wrong or unjust. In opposition to Cicero, then, many others, such as eighteenth-century English poet and philosopher William Godwin, believe humans must be constantly vigilant against bad laws. As Godwin said in 1793:

Laws we sometimes call the wisdom of our ancestors. But this is a strange imposition. It was as frequently the dictate of their passion, of timidity, jealousy, a monopolizing spirit, and a lust of power that knew no bounds. Are we not obliged perpetually to renew and remodel this misnamed wisdom of our ancestors? To correct it by a detection of their ignorance, and a censure of their intolerance?

Lucent Books' *Famous Trials* series showcases trials that exemplify both society's praiseworthy condemnation of universally unacceptable behavior, and its misguided persecution of individuals based on fear and ignorance, as well as trials that leave open the question of whether justice has been done. Each volume begins by setting the scene and providing a historical context to show how society's mores influence the trial process and the verdict.

Each book goes on to present a detailed and lively account of the trial, including liberal use of primary source material such as direct testimony, lawyers' summations, and contemporary and modern commentary. In addition, sidebars throughout the text create a broader context by presenting illuminating details about important points of law, information on key personalities, and important distinctions related to civil, federal, and criminal procedures. Thus, all of the primary and secondary source material included in both the text and the sidebars demonstrates to readers the sources and methods historians use to derive information and conclusions about such events.

Lastly, each *Famous Trials* volume includes one or more of the following comprehensive tools that motivate readers to pursue further reading and research. A timeline allows readers to see the scope of the trial at a glance, annotated bibliographies provide both sources for further research and a thorough list of works consulted, a glossary helps students with unfamiliar words and concepts, and a comprehensive index permits quick scanning of the book as a whole.

The insight of Oliver Wendell Holmes Jr., distinguished Supreme Court justice, exemplifies the theme of the *Famous Trials* series. Taken from *The Common Law*, published in 1881, Holmes remarked: "The life of the law has not been logic, it has been experience." That "experience" consists mainly in how laws are applied in society and challenged in the courts, a process resulting in differing outcomes from one generation to the next. Thus, the *Famous Trials* series encourages readers to examine trials within a broader historical and social context.

Introduction

"Earth Conceal Not the Blood Shed on Thee"
—Inscription on memorial stone,
Bergen-Belsen concentration camp

ADOLF EICHMANN WAS TRIED in Israel in 1961 for crimes committed during World War II. Eichmann, former *Obersturmbannführer* (lieutenant colonel) in Nazi Germany's *Schutzstaffel* (the paramilitary police and security force better known as the SS), was accused of playing a major role in the Holocaust, the systematic murder of 6 million European Jews. The Holocaust was the Third Reich's "final solution" to rid first Europe and then the world of what it considered the "problem" of the Jewish people.

Adolf Eichmann was brought to trial in 1961 by the Israeli government for the atrocities he perpetrated against Jews as a senior Nazi official during World War II.

Adolf Eichmann did not create the "final solution" (though the phrase has been attributed to him), but he was the senior Nazi official concerned solely with the confinement and elimination of the Jews. Eichmann initially coordinated the deportation of Jews from Germany and its occupied territories. Then, when Germany under Adolf Hitler turned from deportation to genocide (mass murder on the basis of race, religion, or ethnic origin), Eichmann organized the

9

transportation of Jews to confinement in eastern Europe, and eventually to death camps.

Eichmann's Career

After joining the SS in 1934, Eichmann rose quickly in responsibility. He made himself an "expert" on Jewish matters, including studying Hebrew and making a brief visit to Palestine on the way to Egypt in 1937. After the March 1938 union of Germany and Austria, Eichmann, an Austrian, was put in charge of the SS unit handling forced Jewish emigration from Austria. Eichmann's office was highly efficient both in looting Jewish possessions and expelling Jews from the country.

In January 1939, inspired by Eichmann's success, the Nazis established a similar office under the Reich Central Security Office (RSHA) for all of German-occupied lands. Eichmann was the logical choice to head this office, the Central Office for Jewish Emigration, usually known by its designation of RSHA Section IV-B-4 (Section IV-D-4 before September 1939). Eichmann headed this section until the end of World War II.

In September 1939 war broke out, and over the next two years, the work of Eichmann's RSHA Section IV-B-4 evolved from expelling Jews from Germany to transporting Jews to death camps in Poland. Eichmann had the resources of the German state to call on for his murderous activities. Based in Berlin, though traveling extensively, Eichmann evolved with the unit, demonstrating ability and enthusiasm for any job he was assigned. He used his often intimidating temperament, and the power of his office, to coordinate the work of mass murder. He made sure trains were available to take Jews to the camps even when this meant diverting needed transportation from the German war effort. He ensured that Jews reported to transportation centers, persuading or intimidating Jewish leaders into cooperating. He even helped plan phases of the actual murder, choosing the method of killing and helping design the layout of Auschwitz, the largest death camp, located in southeastern Poland.

Jews are herded onto railroad cars headed for Auschwitz concentration camp in 1944. Eichmann was so zealous in his determination to eliminate Jews that he would often divert transportation needed for the German war effort.

The Israeli Government and the Capture of Eichmann

The investigation and capture of Nazi war criminals was a major concern of Jewish organizations, and survivors, after World War II. After its creation in 1948, the State of Israel joined the effort to bring fugitives to justice. Eichmann had eluded capture at the end of World War II, but through the continuing efforts of Nazi hunters, he was found in 1959 to be living in Argentina. The Israeli secret police nabbed Eichmann and brought him to stand trial for his crimes.

Israel, a democratic state, maintained that all individuals, however horrible the crimes of which they are accused, are entitled to a fair trial. However, the Israeli government would not have undertaken the long and hard process of bringing Eichmann to justice from Argentina unless they were firmly convinced that he was guilty of a major role in administering the Holocaust. Philosopher and writer Hannah Arendt, a noted observer of the Eichmann trial, questioned Israel's contention that the Eichmann verdict was not predetermined in *Eichmann in Jerusalem:*

> In Israel, as in most other countries, a person appearing in court is deemed innocent until proved guilty. But in the case of Eichmann this was an obvious fiction. If he had not been found guilty before he appeared in Jerusalem, guilty beyond any reasonable doubt, the Israelis would never have dared, or wanted, to kidnap him.[1]

Awaiting trial, Eichmann reads in his jail cell following his capture by Israeli secret police in Argentina.

The prosecution would still have to prove Eichmann's guilt, the trial would still be fair, but the Israeli government always assumed the result would be a verdict of guilty.

The Eichmann Trial as Education

Had the Israelis merely wanted to punish Eichmann, however, killing him in Argentina would have been far easier than capturing him, hiding him for over a week, and then smuggling him back to Israel. The Israeli government had motives other than mere revenge.

For the government, for Holocaust survivors, and for Israelis outraged by the genocide, preserving the memory of the atrocities was of equal or greater importance than proving Eichmann's guilt in a court of law. Israeli young people had little knowledge of the Holocaust, and many older Israelis wanted to forget the horrors of the past. But those Israelis intent on bringing Nazi criminals to justice wanted to ensure that the Holocaust would not be buried in history. They viewed the Eichmann trial as a way to educate Israelis and the world about the evils of totalitarian government run amok. "This trial is not necessary for this defendant," a member of the Israeli Knesset (parliament) said before that body. "This trial is necessary because we need to remind the world of what happened during World War II, something many would like to consign to oblivion." [2]

Though more documentary evidence was collected than was needed to convict Eichmann, chief prosecutor Gideon Hausner wanted to add emotion to dry statistics when presenting his case. Hausner included the testimony of many witnesses, at least twenty-five of whom spoke of the fate of children during the

In order to stir emotions and add meaning to the trial for the younger generation who had not been alive during World War II, chief prosecutor Gideon Hausner (pictured) included the moving testimony of Holocaust survivors.

THE NEW ORDER

In a book published just before the capture of Adolf Eichmann, noted journalist and historian William Shirer described the German "New Order" Eichmann played so great a role in trying to create.

> No comprehensive blueprint for the New Order was ever drawn up, but it is clear from the captured documents and from what took place that Hitler knew very well what he wanted it to be: a Nazi-ruled Europe whose resources would be exploited for the profit of Germany, whose people would be made the slaves of the German master race and whose 'undesirable elements'—above all the Jews, but also many Slavs in the East, especially the intelligentsia among them—would be exterminated.

mass killings. Twenty years after the trial, Hausner said in an interview, "I wanted testimony about the fate of young men and women, so that our own young people would hear what happened."[3] Hausner thought it would be easier for young people to identify with victims their own age. He felt that Israeli youth had failed to identify with what many of their parents and relatives had experienced. Holocaust survivors in Israel had rarely spoken of the horrors that they witnessed. Many survivors assumed that young people brought up in a vigorous new nation would not understand, would ask only "why did you not resist?" Hausner wanted the Holocaust to have meaning for those generations that had not lived through it.

The Meaning of the Trial

The trial of Adolf Eichmann would come to mean different things to different people. For some, it was an opportunity to teach a lesson. For others, it was a cathartic release of painful or repressed memories. For still others, the trial signified long-overdue justice. Isser Harel, the leader of the Israeli effort to capture Eichmann, told his men:

> If we succeed, this will be the first time in history that a court of justice of the Jewish people will judge a man who slaughtered multitudes of Jews. That is why I see in

this action a humane and moral significance that cannot be applied to anything we have ever undertaken before.[4]

The Jewish people survived Hitler, Eichmann, and the Holocaust. Israel was a Jewish state secure and strong enough to grant Eichmann a fundamentally fair trial. Nazi Germany was long gone.

Chapter 1

The Capture of Adolf Eichmann

A DOLF EICHMANN, LIEUTENANT COLONEL IN THE SS, sought power and influence but not a high profile. He vanished from view when World War II ended in 1945 and Nazi atrocities were fully revealed to a horrified world. The Allies had a difficult time researching the details of Eichmann's role in World War II because he was such a shadowy figure. Eichmann's relatively low rank hid the nature and importance of his work, helping to conceal his activities from his victims and from the world at large. Those who searched soon learned that he was the senior Nazi official devoting almost all of his time first to exiling and then to killing the Jews. Eichmann had not created the Holocaust, the organized Nazi murder of 6 million Jewish men, women, and children, but he did play a leading role in carrying it out.

Eichmann Flees Germany at War's End

Eichmann possessed an arrogance and bravado that remained to the end of the war. He told subordinates that "he would leap laughing into his grave because the feeling that he had five million people on his conscience would be for him a source of extraordinary satisfaction."[5] Eichmann was being too modest; he underestimated the number of Jewish dead by a million victims.

In the immediate aftermath of Germany's defeat, Eichmann and his subordinates first planned to escape to the Austrian Alps to fight as guerrillas. This collection of desk officers, who spent

16

the war organizing mass murder but not actually doing any killing, would have made poor soldiers. Eichmann and his men were spared this course of action when a message arrived from SS chief Heinrich Himmler ordering resistance to stop.

Eichmann and one of his aides headed out on their own to attempt to evade Allied forces disguised as Luftwaffe (German air force) enlisted men. Soon captured by American forces, they escaped, but were recaptured. Eichmann was accorded no particular notoriety in the American prisoner-of-war camp, since the Americans did not know his real identity. However, on January 3, 1946, Eichmann's name was mentioned at the Nuremberg war crimes trials as the man who ran the "final solution," the Nazi term for the Holocaust. Eichmann learned he had been mentioned at Nuremberg, and knew the Allies would eventually learn who he was. Two days later he escaped his prison camp through lax security, and headed to a hideout not far from the Bergen-Belsen concentration camp.

For the next four years Eichmann remained in Germany, working as a lumberjack under the name Otto Heninger, though he apparently let some of his relatives believe he was dead. His name was mentioned again and again at war crimes trials, but authorities could not locate him. By 1950, under intensifying threat of detection, Eichmann saw it was time to leave Germany. Through contacts with a clandestine organization of SS veterans, he made his way to Argentina, where his family joined him two years later.

Although Eichmann was named during the Nuremberg war crimes trial in 1946 (pictured) as the man who ran the "final solution," he managed to evade capture until 1960.

By 1956, Eichmann believed that people had lost interest in bringing him to justice. He even granted an interview to a Dutch fascist journalist. (The interview did not lead to his capture, but parts saw print at the time of Eichmann's trial.) In many ways Eichmann was justified in feeling safe. Nazi hunting was less of a concern to Western governments at the height of the cold war, but Jewish survivors, most notably Simon Wiesenthal and his staff, kept up the hunt. However, most Jewish concern was directed to a more immediate problem—the survival of the new State of Israel. Then, in 1957, the phone rang in the office of Isser Harel, chief of Mossad, the soon-to-become-legendary Israeli secret service.

Pinpointing Eichmann

A senior official at Israel's Ministry of Foreign Affairs was on the phone. Harel was struck by the excitement in the voice of the normally restrained official. The two men arranged to meet in a café in a suburb of Tel Aviv, Israel's largest city. The official had startling news for Harel: Adolf Eichmann may have been located. Information passed on by Dr. Fritz Bauer, the public prosecutor of the West German state of Hesse, indicated that Eichmann, by then missing for twelve years, was living in Buenos Aires, the capital of Argentina. On instinct Harel decided that this report, unlike so many false reports in the past, was worth checking out.

Mossad sent an agent to Germany to talk with Dr. Bauer, a German Jew who had spent part of the Nazi era in exile, part in prison in Germany. Bauer explained that he was relaying the report of an informant who lived in Argentina. He claimed that he was giving the information to the Israelis because he was afraid that someone in his own government might warn Eichmann. Bauer kept the original informant's name secret, to protect the man from possible harm from any of Eichmann's supporters or associates.

At the end of the conversation, the Mossad agent asked Bauer who else knew about their meeting. According to Harel, "Bauer replied that he had told only one man about his appeal

EICHMANN'S CAPITAL MISTAKE

Israeli agent Zvi Aharoni, fluent in German, was in charge of interrogating Eichmann before he was taken to Israel. When questioned, Eichmann described his five years hiding in Germany after the war, and his escape to Argentina in 1950. He went on to describe how he kept in contact with his family, and how, when his family joined him in Argentina, he made a fatal mistake. In his 1997 memoir of the capture, *Operation Eichmann*, Aharoni describes this error.

[Eichmann] had corresponded with his wife in Austria for a whole year and a half before she followed him across the Atlantic with the children. Nobody—neither the secret services nor any of the many "Nazi-hunters"—had noticed the extensive exchange of letters at the time. When he was finally reunited with his family, his name was Klement; the others, however, were known as Eichmann. This had turned out to be a capital mistake.

He had not known how to obtain documents for his wife and sons under the false name of Klement. This had been beyond the range of possibilities. Therefore, he had constantly instructed the members of his family to invent stories about themselves and lie to people. Otherwise things would probably have turned out differently. If his sons had called themselves Klement, then neither [the blind man who pointed Bauer and the Mossad in Eichmann's direction or his daughter] would ever have become suspicious.

to the Israelis, a man of standing and of high integrity." [6] Harel later learned that this person was Georg-August Zinn, the prime minister of Hesse, a position roughly equivalent to governor of an American state. Zinn had approved the initial contact with the Israelis, and was kept informed of progress in the operation.

Mossad Begins to Look for Eichmann

Fieldwork to locate Eichmann began with the seemingly simple measure of sending an agent to Buenos Aires to investigate the address Bauer supplied. The agent was asked to find out if Eichmann was living at the address, a house in a suburb just north of Buenos Aires. Discretion was paramount as any carelessness on the agent's part might alert Eichmann and cause him to flee.

The agent soon discovered the house, on an unpaved street, in a poor neighborhood. Struck by its modest appearance, the Mossad investigator questioned the lead because the area did not seem affluent enough for a fugitive senior Nazi. Rumors had been circulating for years that when the leaders of the Third Reich, including Eichmann, saw the war was lost they hid valuables and large sums of money around the world. This treasure was supposedly being used to support them in exile. Even professional intelligence agents tended to share the public perception that senior Nazis would not be living in poor neighborhoods. Initial checks found no evidence to contradict this view. From his low impression of the house and neighborhood, and from these checks, the agent concluded that Eichmann was not living at the house. Additional inquiries among the German community in Argentina yielded no further clues as to Eichmann's whereabouts.

Harel, however, was not sure the initial lead was false. He wanted someone from Mossad to talk directly to Bauer's source. A Mossad representative met with Bauer on January 21, 1958. At this meeting, Bauer, convinced of Mossad's need to meet the source personally as the best way to evaluate the source's honesty and accuracy, revealed the name. He also wrote a letter of introduction for Mossad to use in contacting the source.

The Blind Man's Daughter

Harel decided to send another agent to Argentina, an Israeli police detective bound for Argentina on police business who agreed to undertake the additional mission of contacting Bauer's source. The detective arrived in Buenos Aires in late January 1958.

The police detective was told that Bauer's informant lived in a small town several hundred miles from Buenos Aires. The detective realized a stranger might attract attention, so he sent the informant a telegram asking him to come to the capital. The informant refused, saying that since he did not know the detective, the detective would have to come to him. The detective agreed, and headed out of the capital.

On meeting the informant and presenting Bauer's letter, the detective learned some facts about the informant and his family. The man was a blind German Jew who was sympathetic to Israel. As a young man during World War II he had been confined in a German concentration camp. His parents had been among Eichmann's victims. Surviving the war, the man moved to Argentina. His wife was not Jewish, and his daughter, though half-Jewish, was the type of blond the Nazis considered the "ideal" physical type. It was through his attractive daughter's youthful romances that the man became suspicious of Eichmann's presence in Argentina.

His daughter had dated a young man calling himself Nicolas Eichmann. Nicolas had openly expressed his views with the family, whose surname did not appear to be Jewish, that the Germans should have finished the job of killing all European Jewry during World War II. Nicolas also explained that he lacked a regional German accent because his father served in different locations during the war. One day the blind man's wife or daughter, he did not recall which, read a story about a war crimes trial in Germany mentioning a man named Adolf Eichmann. The informant thought that "Nicolas Eichmann, who's so sorry that the Nazis didn't manage to wipe out all the Jews, must be the son of Adolf Eichmann."[7]

Eichmann's son, Nicolas (pictured), dated the daughter of a blind Jewish man. The man later helped pinpoint Eichmann's hideout.

The informant checked further. He and his daughter made two trips into Buenos Aires, trying to find where the Eichmanns lived and to meet the head of the family. The informant went on to say that

It was then that we recalled an episode to which we had not attributed any importance at the beginning: my daughter and Nicolas had been writing to each other since we moved here, but he never told her where he lived; he asked her to send her letters to the address of a mutual friend.[8]

The daughter added further details:

When we went to Buenos Aires I asked a friend to help me find his house. I knocked at the door and it was opened by a woman. I asked her in German if this was the house of the Eichmann family. Her reply did not come immediately, and during the pause a middle-aged man wearing glasses came and stood beside her. I asked him if Nick was home. He said no, Nick was working overtime. I asked if he was Mr. Eichmann. . . . He said he was but only after some hesitation.[9]

The detective never found out why the man willingly confirmed he was Eichmann, since he was living under an assumed name. And, it was never mentioned whether the blind man's daughter ever saw Nicolas Eichmann again.

The detective was sufficiently interested to ask the informant to check further, as the Buenos Aires residence had been vacated when the detective arrived. The informant agreed, but the only significant lead he found did not become clear until later. The former residence had two gas meters, one in the name of Klement or Klements. By the start of 1959, with the detective long since returned to Israel and his regular police duties, Mossad permitted contact with the informant, seeming to yield no further information, to end.

Bauer's Second Lead to Eichmann

Bauer visited Israel in 1959 and met Isser Harel. At this meeting, Bauer passed on new information, from a different informant, that again supported the notion that Eichmann was in Argentina. According to this source, Eichmann appeared to be using the name Ricardo Klement, the same name the first informant had discovered on the gas meter in the vacated house. With this lead, Harel tried to get Bauer to divulge more information about his source. As Harel later recalled, his answer was not very fruitful:

> It was absolutely impossible to make Bauer reveal any details whatsoever about the new source. But I realized immediately that this was the turning point and we were now steering toward the open road. Only one question bothered me, and I asked for clarification: How can I be sure there is no connection, either direct or indirect, between the new source and [the first informant]? Bauer's reply was unequivocal: There is not, and there never could be, any connection between the two.[10]

Mossad's Plan

Mossad obtained photos of Ricardo Klement and determined that his size and age were possibly those of Eichmann. His appearance reflected the physical changes likely to have

---

An identity card issued to Eichmann in Buenos Aires under the alias Ricardo Klement contains a photo of the aging Nazi.

---

occurred in Eichmann in the fifteen years since the end of the war, despite efforts to change his appearance, including growing a mustache. Mossad strongly believed that Klement was Eichmann. However, in the words of one agent involved in the capture, "We can't be one hundred percent sure until we've got him." [11] Once in Israel, Mossad planned to confirm his identity through several Israelis who had met Eichmann.

Harel felt he had enough evidence to authorize the capture of Ricardo Klement, but he wanted to make sure the Israelis had legal justification to remove Klement from foreign soil and try him in Israel. Israeli judicial experts confirmed that trying the suspect in Israel would be legal; the Israelis understood that taking Eichmann from Argentina would violate that nation's sovereignty. With Israeli prime minister David Ben-Gurion's approval, the plan was put into action.

A team of Israeli agents headed by Harel was sent to Argentina. (Harel would not be present for the actual capture, but was in Buenos Aires in charge of the overall mission.) The Israeli agents began to study Klement's habits, to make specific plans for his capture and transportation to Israel. They selected "safe houses," alternative places to hold the suspect until he could be moved from Argentina. The agents were cautious not to alert landlords or neighbors to unusual activity at these rented houses. The Israeli team included a doctor to take care of Klement and to sedate him for the trip to the airport.

In the event that the Argentine police discovered and intercepted the kidnapping,

Israeli prime minister David Ben-Gurion approved the plan to capture and transport Eichmann to Israel for trial.

EICHMANN'S CAPTURE AND
ISRAELI INTELLIGENCE

Zvi Aharoni led the Mossad effort which located Adolf Eichmann in Argentina, and he was a member of the team of Israeli agents which actually captured Eichmann. Both efforts were under the overall direction of Isser Harel, director of Mossad. In an introduction to Aharoni's 1997 memoir of the capture, retired Israeli general Meir Amit, Harel's successor as director of Mossad, writes of the effects Eichmann's capture had on the Israeli intelligence community.

> The operation to capture Eichmann in Argentina was regarded by the Israeli intelligence community with mixed feelings. . . . There was no doubt that for many months, largely as a result of Operation Eichmann, the main efforts of Mossad were diverted from its prime target [intelligence on Israel's hostile Arab neighbors].

> In [any] event, it became clear that Operation Eichmann was justified, not just because its objective was of major national importance—capturing the man who was responsible, almost directly, for the operation of the Nazi extermination machinery and for causing the deaths of millions of Jews. But, in addition, the successful planning of this operation, the unfailing determination to see it through, the great resourcefulness shown by the operations in the field, and its clean execution, resulted in increased respect for the Israeli intelligence community in general, and Mossad in particular. There is not the slightest doubt that the immense regard for the intelligence community generated by this operation, together with the recognition of the extraordinary dimensions of its operational capacity, strengthened Israeli intelligence and contributed to its subsequent success.

Harel ordered one of his men to handcuff himself to Eichmann and throw away the key. One or two other men would stay in the area to report on what happened. The designated agent was ordered, over his protests, to tell the police he was part of a volunteer effort led by Isser Harel to capture Adolf Eichmann and turn him over to Argentine authorities.

Harel and his men even helped plan a special El Al (Israeli state airline) flight from Israel to Buenos Aires and back. The flight would bring an Israeli delegation to help celebrate the 150th anniversary of Argentine independence in May 1960. The plane would carry Eichmann back to Israel.

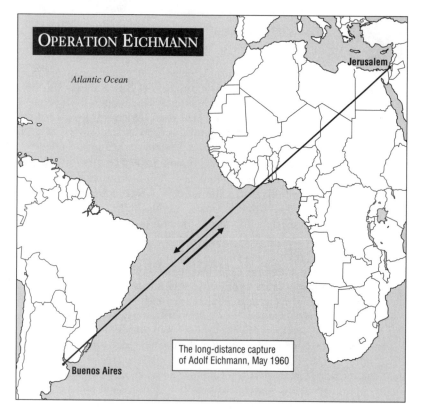

The long-distance capture of Adolf Eichmann, May 1960

Klement's Capture

The Klement family was living in another working-class Buenos Aires suburb, at some distance from the one first investigated. Klement held a job in Buenos Aires, taking a train and a bus home every evening. He usually returned about 7:00 P.M., walking the final few hundred yards to his house. The house was somewhat isolated, near a railroad embankment; there were, however, neighbors. Fortunately May is late fall below the equator. Klement would be walking home in the dark.

On the evening of May 11, the capture car was sitting some distance from Klement's house, facing west, opposite the direction of the suspect's approach. A second car faced south under a nearby railroad bridge. Its lights would be in Klement's eyes as he walked from the bus stop. He would not see the second car until it was too late.

Klement, normally a man of regular habits, was late getting off the bus that evening. One of the agents, concerned, stepped from the second car to scout the street when he saw a man walking in the darkness. He scrambled back to the second car to signal his comrades to turn on the lights. The agents in the first car had also seen the target. They noticed the suspect had a hand in his pocket, and they assumed he might be carrying a gun. The agent designated to perform the capture walked towards Klement. Thunder in the background provided ominous sound effects.

"Un momentito, señor," the agent called. Klement took a step backwards and froze. When the agent reached for him, they both ended up falling into the mud. The suspect shouted but was quickly silenced. A second agent helped get him into the car, which immediately drove off. He was gagged, tied up, and blindfolded in the car. Klement was told, by an agent who "spoke one sentence to him in German, using terms which were undoubtedly familiar to the captive: 'If you don't keep still, you'll be shot.'"[12]

Eichmann was intercepted by Israeli agents on May 11, 1960, as he walked from a bus stop to his modest home.

A CRUCIAL LESSON

The introduction to Mossad director Isser Harel's *The House on Garibaldi Street* contains a description of the effect of Eichmann's trial.

> After Eichmann's public trial . . . a small delegation came to see [Isser] Harel in his office. These were the remaining Jewish fighters of the Warsaw Ghetto uprising. In tears they thanked Harel for bringing Eichmann to justice. "Before the trial nobody wanted to hear of the Holocaust" they explained. Now the legacy of the Holocaust would be very different, after the horrors, the plans and the machinations of this satanic genocide were fully exposed by its leading architect. The young generation in Israel learned through the trial a crucial lesson on its history and heritage, a lesson which is now passed down through the generations.

On arrival at the designated safe house, the suspect was examined, questioned, and found to meet the Israelis' description of Eichmann. Though he first gave his name as Ricardo Klement, the man knew almost automatically Eichmann's Nazi Party membership number. When one of the captors intentionally misread Eichmann's SS identification number, the suspect corrected the number. Finally, in response to yet another question about his name, he admitted, "I am Adolf Eichmann." [13] A few days later, Eichmann signed a statement that he would voluntarily stand trial in Israel.

By May 23, 1960, Eichmann was safely in Israel and convincingly identified by Jewish witnesses who had known Eichmann during his days in Vienna. On that date, Israeli prime minister David Ben-Gurion made a startling announcement to the Knesset, the Israeli parliament: "It is my duty to inform you that a short time ago the security services apprehended one of the most infamous Nazi criminals, Adolf Eichmann. . . . Adolf Eichmann is already imprisoned in this country, and will soon be brought to trial in Israel." [14]

Harel later wrote, somewhat poetically,

> The news flashed from the Knesset to the entire nation of Israel, to the tortured who had survived the murder

factory, to the bereaved who has lost so many dear ones. This reconfirmation of the rule of law heartened them and renewed their faith in justice.

And the news reached the far corners of the earth, imbuing all decent people with a feeling of respect; and it carried with it a clear warning to the murderers of the Jewish people, hiding in their holes, who thought that the years would whiten their sins and silence the cry of the blood they had shed, and that none would come any more to make them face judgement for the millions they had slain in their criminal frenzy.[15]

Israel is a democracy with an explicit code of law. Under its judicial system, a defendant is presumed innocent until proven guilty, Eichmann would be tried in a court of law with legal representation. The Israeli prosecutors would have to prove Eichmann's guilt, his willing complicity in the murder of 6 million Jews. With the eyes of the world upon them, the prosecutors would have to prepare their case well.

Chapter 2

Preparing the Case

HAVING CAPTURED ADOLF EICHMANN, and announced to a stunned world that the chief planner and coordinator of the Holocaust was a prisoner in Israel, the Israeli government now had to prepare for Eichmann's trial. Israeli authorities had determined that Israeli law allowed Eichmann to be tried in Israel. International law and practice also allowed Israel to try Eichmann. In the words of a UN document,

> According to generally recognised doctrine . . . the right to punish war crimes is not confined to the State whose nationals have suffered or on whose territory the offence took place, but is possessed by any independent State whatsoever, just as is the right to punish the offence of piracy. This doctrine . . . has received the support of the United Nations War Crimes Commission and is generally accepted as sound.[16]

However, Israel had yet to gauge the attitudes of the world regarding the means of Eichmann's capture. Would other nations object to Israel's methods?

World Reaction

Dealing with world reaction to Eichmann's capture, Israel paid particular attention to the attitudes of the three countries—Argentina, West Germany, and East Germany—that might have been expected to argue that the Eichmann trial be conducted in their courts.

ISRAEL'S POSTWAR RELATIONS WITH GERMANY

In the early years of the State of Israel, well before Eichmann's capture, the question of how to remember the Holocaust was linked to what sort of relationship the new state wanted to maintain with the Federal Republic of Germany. Was it the same nation that had so grievously harmed the Jews? Israeli journalist and historian Tom Segev, in his book *1949: The First Israelis*, writes on this question.

The awareness of the Holocaust and the means of preserving its memory were still in their embryonic stages—at this time they reflected hatred and vindictiveness, not yet a national mythology of heroic resistance, which characterized Israel's later attitude toward the Holocaust. "We must inculcate hatred for Germans in our young children and in their offspring to come," asserted an article in the evening paper *Yediot Aharonot.* "Vengeance must come, and it will come when we are stronger." The first Israelis did not quite know how to deal with the problem. The slightest hint of a possible connection with Germany, and especially visits by Germans to Israel, aroused violent reactions in the press. . . . While still searching for the proper way of commemorating the Holocaust, a kibbutz [communal farming community] was established and named Buchenwald, after the concentration camp. Later it was renamed Netser Sereni, after [a Jewish] agent who was dropped behind the German lines during the war and perished. In the spring of 1949 "The Seven Dwarfs from Auschwitz," two brothers and five sisters, Hungarian-born survivors of the death camps, who were dwarfs, toured the country singing and dancing, before full houses. At the same time, the Knesset [Israeli parliament] debated laws against genocide as well as a law to bring Nazis and their accomplices to justice.

The storm first broke over how the Israelis captured Eichmann. A few days after Eichmann's capture, Ben-Gurion wrote Argentine president Arturo Frondizi:

As a result of the capture of the Nazi war criminal Adolf Eichmann and his transfer to Israel, misunderstandings may arise in the relations between the Republic of Argentina and the State of Israel, and I therefore regard it as my duty to send you this direct message. . . .

During the Second World War this man Eichmann was the person directly responsible for the execution of

Hitler's orders for the "final solution" of the Jewish problem in Europe, i.e., the murder of every single Jew on whom the Nazis could lay their hands throughout the territories of Europe which they had occupied at the time. Six million of our people were murdered in Europe, and it was Eichmann who organized this mass murder, on a gigantic and unprecedented scale, throughout Europe.

I need not explain to you, Mr. President, what it means for any people on earth to be the victims of such a satanic murder campaign, and what profound scars such an experience must leave in a people's soul. . . .

I do not underestimate the seriousness of the formal violation of Argentine law committed by those who found Eichmann, but I am convinced that very few people anywhere can fail to understand their feelings and appreciate the supreme moral validity of their act. . . . Though I do not question for a moment the duty of every State to respect its neighbour's laws . . . yet we can appreciate the overriding motives whose tremendous moral and emotional force underlay the determination to find the chief murderer and to bring him, with his consent, to Israel.[17]

Ben-Gurion was unsure of Argentinian sympathies, but at least one Argentine newspaper seemed to support the Israelis:

How can we not admire a group of brave men who have during the years endangered their lives in searching throughout the world for these criminals and yet had the honesty to deliver him up for trial by judicial tribunals instead of being impelled by an impulse of revenge and finishing him off on the spot.[18]

Argentina did not request Eichmann's extradition, but did file a complaint concerning the violation of their national sovereignty with the UN Security Council. Israel admitted the violation and apologized to Argentina. With Argentina satisfied, the Security

The Argentine ambassador addresses the UN Security Council, asking its members to declare that Israel violated Argentina's national sovereignty when they captured Eichmann. The council chose not to take action after Israel admitted the violation and apologized.

Council took no action. The method of Eichmann's capture soon faded as a topic of discussion. Most people seemed to find it unnecessary to examine the legal case for Israeli jurisdiction, and accepted the view expressed in an American newspaper editorial that a "sense of proportion counsels that the human aspect of the Eichmann case take precedence over protocol." [19]

German Reaction

Germany had been divided into two countries at the end of World War II. Neither state, however, requested Eichmann's extradition. East Germany made no public comment on the case. West Germany was supportive, and responded favorably to Israel's requests for assistance, primarily to validate documents and to locate witnesses. The West German press supported this position. A major German newspaper summarized the views of the West German media in writing that

Adolf Eichmann has found his hunters and, above all, his judges. . . . It is not for us to question the Israeli authorities, who were able to put their hands on Eichmann, as to the methods of the arrest. We have no right to cite legalistic aspects of the question. In the last analysis, this would only serve to quieten [sic] our conscience. One who has brutally placed himself above the law and unscrupulously transgressed every canon of nature has, it seems to us, forgone any right to any kind of solidarity. We in this country, who were unable to bring Eichmann to trial in our courts, should now have confidence in Israel's jurisdiction: justice, not vengeance, will rule the day.[20]

Most of the world seemed to support Israel's actions, and agreed that Israel was legally allowed to try Eichmann. Under international legal principles and statutes, states have a legal right and responsibility to punish war crimes and crimes against humanity. No other state with a possible claim on Eichmann chose to exercise this claim.

Defending the Fairness of Eichmann's Trial

Eichmann would receive an appropriate trial. However, would Eichmann receive a fair trial? Gideon Hausner, the newly appointed Israeli attorney general (the chief prosecuting attorney for the government of Israel, not the equivalent of the cabinet-level U.S. attorney general) and Eichmann's prosecutor, stated that

We faced a formidable task; we were bound to present an overwhelming legal case to sweep away all juridical doubts, and we had to offer an immaculate factual case to establish beyond a shadow of doubt the truth of our allegations. Only after clearing the ground of all skeptical objections and lingering doubts could we aspire to establish the complete structure of our accusation.[21]

Concerns about fairness ended when people saw how the defendant was treated. Eichmann had the right to legal counsel of his own choosing; he selected Dr. Robert Servatius, a German

German lawyer Robert Servatius purchases his ticket to Israel, where he headed to defend Eichmann.

lawyer with experience defending accused war criminals. Israel not only partly funded the defense, but the Knesset passed a special law enabling Servatius, a non-Israeli, to argue before an Israeli court. German newspapers praised Eichmann's treatment: "Since his capture, Eichmann has been subjected to orderly proceedings and all the legal means have been made available to him for an adequate defense." [22]

Multiple Goals

Establishing Eichmann's guilt was only one goal of the trial, perhaps not even the primary goal. During the trial, Ben-Gurion would write that "It is not the punishment that is the main thing here but the fact that the trial is taking place, and is taking place in Jerusalem." [23] Ben-Gurion saw two goals for the trial outside of its obvious judicial purposes. One goal was to remind the world of the Holocaust and what Ben-Gurion considered the world's obligations to support the only Jewish state on earth. The second was to impress the lessons of the Holocaust on the Israelis, especially on the younger generation. Thus, the three-judge panel that would, according to Israeli law, decide Eichmann's guilt or innocence, was only one of several audiences for the prosecution's case.

There was a clear need in 1960 and 1961 to educate many Israelis about the Holocaust, especially younger Israelis born in Israel. "Sabra" is the term for native-born Israelis, including those born before Israel's 1948 independence in what was then Palestine (not to be confused with the term's current meaning as an independent state for Palestinian Arabs). The Sabras had grown up in a vibrant, developing, but vulnerable country. Israel

Curious Israeli youngsters watch as people arrive for the first day of the Eichmann trial. Ben-Gurion believed that one of the hearing's main goals should be to teach the lessons of the Holocaust to the younger generation of Israelis.

was surrounded by enemies intent on its destruction. The country's survival was never assured.

There was one key difference, however, between the crises faced by the Jews in Israel and those faced by the Jews in Nazi-occupied Europe. The Israelis always felt that they could defend themselves, that they could strike back at their enemies. Many Sabras found it difficult to understand how the European Jews could have accepted their treatment without resisting. These feelings caused resentment, and the Holocaust became a troubling subject to discuss.

The Holocaust was almost ignored in Israel. Teachers did not know how to teach it in school. Many of these teachers, in fact, were Holocaust survivors, and the memory was too painful. Survivors did not want to talk about what they had gone through, unwilling to relive the horror. Guilt feelings over surviving, when so many others had died, plagued survivors. The young, in particular, were not willing to listen. They could not understand a world so foreign to their own. The contemptuous nickname "pieces of soap" was applied to survivors, the term stemming from reports that Nazis had made soap from the bodies of Holocaust victims. The question in the minds of the Sabras remained "Why did they not resist?" This attitude towards the Holocaust was still prevalent in Israel when Isser Harel and his Mossad agents captured Eichmann.

Ben-Gurion's Role

By 1960 David Ben-Gurion had been prime minister of Israel, except for brief periods, since Israel's independence in 1948. Emigrating from Poland well before World War II, Ben-Gurion was a leader of the Jewish community in Palestine throughout the Holocaust. Establishing an independent Israel was Ben-Gurion's overriding concern before 1948. He once even said, "The disaster facing European Jewry is not my business," [24] though this comment arose not from lack of sympathy but from a realization that little could be done.

In 1960, as preparations for the Eichmann trial were under way, consciousness of the Holocaust had already begun to fade

Prime Minister Ben-Gurion, determined not to let the memories and lessons of the Holocaust fade from people's minds, urged prosecutor Gideon Hausner to use the trial as a way to educate Israel and the world by employing the emotional testimonies of Holocaust survivors.

among younger Israelis and in the world at large. Perhaps wondering if he and the other leaders of the Yishuv (the pre-1948 Jewish community in Palestine) could have done more to prevent the disaster, Ben-Gurion was determined to educate Israel and the world about the Holocaust. The one exception to Israeli democratic procedures noted in reports of the trial was that from time to time Ben-Gurion issued instructions to Gideon Hausner to stress educational aspects. Prosecutors are supposed to be independent of political considerations. Hausner, however, shared the prime minister's desire to inform and educate as well as determine Eichmann's guilt in court. Both wanted the trial to be more than a dry presentation of documents. The way to achieve this, the way to put flesh and soul to the dry statistics, was through the testimony of witnesses.

Identifying Witnesses

The Nazis had been careful to document their activities, including the murder of the Jews. Eichmann's office had burned its records at war's end, but to little effect, as they were for the most part copies of records filed and sent to other Reich offices, whose records were seized by the Allies. The Israelis accumulated a vast amount of those documents, from their own government and private archives and from investigations in Europe and elsewhere. Near the end of the investigation, Hausner asked Dr. Robert M. W. Kempner, the assistant U.S. chief counsel at the 1945 Nuremberg trials and an expert on Nazi documentation, to take a look at what the Israelis had. Kempner reported that Israel's material "surpassed by far that which was known to the prosecution authorities at Nuremberg." These documents alone could have convicted Eichmann. As Hausner put it, "A fraction of [the documents] would have sufficed to get Eichmann sentenced ten times over." [25]

However, Hausner and Ben-Gurion wanted the world to hear the testimonies of those who had survived the horror in which Eichmann played such a pivotal role. Hausner asserted that "We needed more than a conviction; we needed a living record of a gigantic human and national disaster, though it could never be more than a feeble record of the real events. . . . I decided that the case would rest on two main pillars instead of one: both documents and oral evidence." [26]

Each witness would be asked to tell his or her own small portion of the Holocaust story. Together they would present a human picture of the Holocaust to accompany the overwhelming documentary evidence.

Many of the witnesses, however, were reluctant to talk in open court. Some wanted to forget. Others were afraid they would not be believed. Some had actually been disbelieved when they emerged from hiding after the war. Yet Hausner successfully appealed to their sense of duty and to their deep-seated desire to tell their story to the world. Hausner eventually called 112 witnesses, mostly Jewish survivors of the Holocaust.

ISRAELI POLICE INVESTIGATION PROCEDURES

Captain Avner W. Less, a German-speaking member of the Israeli police, was the man who actually conducted Adolf Eichmann's pre-trial interrogation in Israel. Selections from the three hundred hours of interrogation were published in 1983. In his introduction to the published transcript, Less described the procedures the Israeli police follow in investigations, and the exception made for the Eichmann case.

> The [Israeli] police, who are not under the authority of the Attorney General, conduct the investigation from beginning to end, independently and in the framework of their own guidelines. The police officer conducting the investigation does not have the function or powers of an examining magistrate [the investigation officer in continental Europe]. After the police investigation has been completed, the whole dossier goes to the Attorney General's office, which examines it for errors and inconsistencies, and then presents the court with a written indictment.

The police do not work under the control of the prosecution, but, as in the United States, the prosecution is sometimes kept informed. Less goes on to write that,

> Throughout the police investigation of Eichmann, we worked in close association with Attorney General Gideon Hausner [and his staff]. . . . They had to familiarize themselves with the complex material very quickly; the government insisted on holding the trial in the near future, and so the indictment had to be drawn up in a hurry.

Interrogating Eichmann

The Israeli police force, operating independently of Hausner and the rest of the prosecution team, conducted the investigation and interrogation of Eichmann. Israeli law assumes that the police will be more objective if they can act independently of the prosecution. A special police unit called Bureau 06 was formed to investigate the case.

The process began informally. Acting against orders, the agent who grabbed Eichmann talked with him, though this conversation was not brought out in the trial. The agent's primary observation of Eichmann was that it was impossible to find common human ground with the man. Eichmann would express genuine concern about his family. Then, with no emotion at all,

he would discuss his activities in pursuit of the "final solution."
The agent later wrote that

> never, not once, did the man convey anything but the
> feeling that everything he had done was absolutely
> appropriate. Not nice, necessarily, or even reasonable,
> but absolutely correct in context. There was a job to do
> and he did it.[27]

The agent observed that Eichmann vigorously defended his
position that a solution to the "Jewish problem" had to be found.
Eichmann, however, shaded the truth concerning his involvement to lessen his own responsibility.

During formal interrogation, and questioning at his trial,
Eichmann never admitted ultimate responsibility for any of his
actions. He showed a remarkable memory for details of his early
life, for example, giving lengthy answers to questions about early
family life. However, he seemed to forget a lot about his more
memorable World War II activities. Gideon Hausner later wrote
that "[Eichmann's] earlier feats of memory had been so extraordinary that no one could seriously believe he was capable of such
remarkable lapses."[28] The police noted this same tendency
towards selective memory.

Eichmann maintained that he was only following orders, that
he could not act on his own, or that he knew nothing, repeating
the rationalizations of other accused Nazi war criminals. He
claimed that actions not in response to direct orders were taken
by others, including subordinates who were somehow both able
and willing to act on their own initiative. During interrogation
Eichmann claimed he never acted on his own. He never stopped
to think about what he was doing, nor about the goals he was
supporting. The reasons behind the orders were not to be questioned by subordinates like himself.

Early in the investigation, chief police interrogator Avner
Less asked Eichmann about a well-known tenet of Adolf
Hitler's anti-Semitic doctrine. This particular claim was one of
Hitler's espoused political beliefs as well as an aspect of Nazi
indoctrination familiar to most Germans.

LESS: Did you know that Hitler accused the Jews of causing the defeat of Germany in the First World War?

EICHMANN: At that time I belonged to the category of people who form no opinions of their own.[29]

Eichmann claimed he was incapable of exercising individual initiative. At one point, Less asked Eichmann to explain documents ordering the deportation to Auschwitz of specified Jewish women:

Chief police interrogator Avner Less testifies in the trial that during his interrogation of the defendant, Eichmann repeatedly refused to take personal responsibility for his actions.

LESS: You have claimed that you never took a hand in the fate of individual Jews. But these documents speak for themselves. They show you had full powers.

EICHMANN: . . . They were not personal decisions. If I had not been sitting there, someone else would have had to make exactly the same decisions on the basis of instructions, regulations, and orders of the higher-ups. I wasn't expected to make any decisions at all.[30]

Personal initiative was always shown by others, never by Eichmann. Asked about stripping deported Romanian Jews of their citizenship when they crossed the Romanian border, Eichmann replied, "The Foreign Office must have imposed that condition. In such matters, the Foreign Office always took precedence."[31]

Sometimes Eichmann claimed to know nothing about particular events. At one point in the interrogation, Eichmann was asked about the forced march of Jews from Hungary to Auschwitz after the rail system had been destroyed:

LESS: On November 16, 1944, a group of highly placed German guests arrived in Budapest [Hungary]. . . . On the road . . . they were witnesses to the horrible foot march. The road was heaped with corpses. . . .

EICHMANN: I assure you, I know nothing about those . . . those heaps of corpses on the road.[32]

Eichmann apparently wanted the interrogator to believe that he had not even heard rumors about such a sloppy violation of his neat and efficient transportation program. At the trial, it came out that Eichmann had ordered the march, and had done so in violation of SS chief Heinrich Himmler's wish to end the deportation of Jews.

Mostly, Eichmann claimed his actions were in response to direct orders:

LESS: Am I to understand that after rolling stock had been requisitioned and you knew how many cars were available, you would set the quota of Jews to be deported from the occupied countries accordingly?

EICHMANN: Well, yes, but . . . it wasn't me. . . . I definitely had orders from the Reichsführer [Himmler].[33]

All of Eichmann's testimony from these interrogations was introduced by the prosecution as evidence during the trial.

Hausner Decides the Charges

Hausner, as chief prosecutor, had the responsibility of deciding how Eichmann would be charged. He had to decide whether the charge sheet would be limited, specifying particular acts about which Israeli evidence was strongest. This would have simplified the legal arguments. "But then," Hausner later wrote, "I would have had to limit my evidence to [the specified] incidents alone and thus miss the point of the trial: the covering of the whole Jewish disaster."[34]

The alternative was to go with broader charges "imputing to Eichmann responsibility for all his widely ranging criminal activities and using particular instances as proof of his exceptional malice."[35] This approach had disadvantages, as it would require broad, comprehensive proof to substantiate prosecution claims. It ran the legal risk that, during the trial, some of Hausner's evidence would seem irrelevant to Eichmann's guilt or innocence. It also ran the political risk that if Eichmann were acquitted on some of the major charges, even if it did not affect the final result, the public image would be that his guilt and responsibility were overstated.

Hausner selected the broader approach, charging Eichmann with guilt for the Holocaust in all the occupied territories. Hausner cited two legal reasons: In addition to wanting the clear opportunity to cover the entire Jewish disaster, he knew Eichmann was head of the RSHA subsection charged with carrying out the final solution. It is a common principle of law that every active participant in a crime is responsible for the results of the crime. If Eichmann's position was as central as the prosecution charged, then he shared responsibility for the entire Holocaust.

The general approach to charging Eichmann was selected. The specific charges would be drafted and read at the start of the trial.

Conclusions of the Investigation

Throughout the interrogation Eichmann tried to present himself as an ordinary bureaucrat. Admittedly he was doing extraordinary work, but he claimed to be so locked into an inflexible structure that he could do nothing either to change the murderous work or his role in the work. However, by the time they read the formal transcripts of Eichmann's interrogation, the prosecution already had a different view of Eichmann. Though the police operate independently of the prosecution in Israel, the prosecution was kept abreast of the information being gathered, including Eichmann's testimony and the massive documentary evidence collected on the Holocaust (and Eichmann's role in its

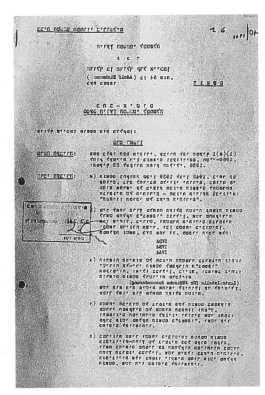

The first page of the indictment of Eichmann by chief prosecutor Hausner. In order to show the huge scope of atrocities he committed during the war, Hausner chose to charge Eichmann with wide-ranging liability for the Holocaust.

SELECTIONS FROM NAZIS AND NAZI COLLABORATORS (PUNISHMENT) LAW

The Trial of Adolf Eichmann, case number 40/61 in the District Court of Jerusalem, was prosecuted under Sections 1 and 3 of the Nazis and Nazi Collaborators (Punishment) Law of 1950. The texts of Section 1, the primary legal basis for the case against Eichmann, follows:

1(a) A person who has committed one of the following offences:

(1) done, during the period of the Nazi regime, in an enemy country, an act constituting a crime against the Jewish people;

(2) done, during the period of the Nazi regime, in an enemy country, an act constituting a crime against humanity;

(3) done, during the period of the Second World War, in an enemy country, an act constituting a war crime,

is liable to the death penalty.

(b) in this section;

"crimes against the Jewish people" means any of the following acts, committed with intent to destroy the Jewish people in whole or in part:

(1) killing Jews;

(2) causing serious bodily or mental harm to Jews;

(3) placing Jews in living conditions calculated to bring about their physical destruction;

(4) imposing measures intended to prevent births among Jews;

(5) forcible transferring [of] Jewish children to another national or religious group;

(6) destroying or desecrating Jewish religious or cultural assets or values;

(7) inciting to hatred of Jews;

"crime against humanity" means any of the following acts:

murder, extermination, enslavement, starvation or deportation and other inhumane acts committed against any civilian population, and persecution on national, racial, religious or political grounds;

"war crime" means any of the following acts:

murder, ill-treatment or deportation to forced labour or for any other purpose, of civilian population of or in occupied territory; murder or ill-treatment of prisoners or persons on the seas; killing of hostages; plunder of public or private property; wanton destruction of cities, towns or villages; and devastation not justified by military necessity.

implementation.) The prosecution had concluded that Eichmann was anything but a rubber-stamp bureaucrat. Hausner's team knew that Eichmann was inflexible only as to his goal, killing as many Jews as possible. They knew that he did what was necessary to reach his goal. The prosecutors knew that Eichmann showed characteristic initiative and creativity in pursuit of cold-blooded murder. The prosecution now had to prove this in court.

Chapter 3

The Trial Opens

ADOLF EICHMANN WALKED TO HIS bulletproof glass cubicle a little before 9:00 A.M. on April 11, 1961, eleven months to the day after his capture in Argentina. "The man in the glass booth," he would come to be known. "As [Eichmann] silently entered the packed courtroom there was an audible gasp," [36] chief prosecutor Gideon Hausner later noted. Eichmann had been seen by only a few people since his arrival in Israel. Not even Hausner had seen Eichmann before trial began.

In his book on the trial, Hausner wrote that "externally there was little to indicate his nature." [37] Eichmann's eyes would flash intently, almost angrily, at times, especially later in the trial when his testimony was contradicted during cross-examination, but otherwise he appeared gray and colorless.

The Trial Setting

The bulletproof glass behind which Eichmann sat protected him from a violent attack, however unlikely, from anyone in the courtroom. Eichmann had been kept in secure facilities during interrogation and while awaiting trial. He was guarded to prevent rescue and to ensure his safety from misguided vengeance, or from Nazis who might be seeking to silence him. A guard had been in his cell at all times, to prevent suicide. Authorities had intercepted several letters directly or indirectly urging this action, including one that concealed half a razor blade under the stamps. Eichmann may have been in no danger, but the Israelis were taking no chances.

Eichmann came to be known as "the man in the glass booth" during his trial because of the bulletproof glass cubicle that protected him from any would-be assassins. Eichmann's attorney, Servatius, appears in the lower left foreground.

The Building and the Courtroom

Jerusalem's nearly completed cultural center was borrowed for the trial. High metal fences surrounded the building during its use as a court. It was heavily guarded; visitors were frisked and their bags searched.

The courtroom was located in a temporarily converted auditorium. Also prepared were judges' chambers, offices for the defense and prosecution staffs, court archives, and a secure holding area to house Eichmann when court was not in session. A large hall beneath the courtroom, which later became a municipal library, was set aside for the press.

At one end of the courtroom the highest tier of a raised platform was reserved for the three judges, who sat behind a wood-paneled table. Court stenographers, keeping the official records of the trial, sat to the sides of the judges. Translators sat in front and on a lower level. The official court language was Hebrew, Israel's national language. Many witnesses and Eichmann himself spoke in German. All proceedings were available in both these languages, as well as English, French, and Yiddish (a German dialect spoken by Jews from eastern Europe). Despite the best intentions of the Israelis, however, the translations varied in quality. At times the judges, who spoke German as well as Hebrew, had to step in and directly supervise the translation into and from German.

Eichmann's glass cubicle was in the left forefront of the courtroom, the witness box in the right forefront, facing each other. Literally as well as symbolically the accused would be confronted by his accusers. Defense and prosecution tables faced the judges.

The Eichmann trial took place in this building, a nearly completed cultural center in Jerusalem.

Eichmann, at left in his glass cubicle, stands to face the panel of three judges who were to decide his fate. On the back wall is the menorah, an ancient Jewish symbol which is also the state seal of Israel.

The Judges

Every person in the courtroom, including Adolf Eichmann, rose to their feet as the three black-robed judges entered and took their seats. On the wall behind them was the seal of the State of Israel, the seven-branched candelabra called a menorah, a Jewish symbol since ancient times. Eichmann, on trial for his role in a dead regime that had tried to destroy the Jewish people, performed the gesture honoring the representatives of a democratic Jewish state.

The Israeli Judicial System

The Israeli judicial system evolved from the English system in place in 1948 at independence. English common law is often cited in Israeli courts, as are legal precedents from the American system. The resulting system contains many elements familiar to Americans, including the need for the prosecutor to prove a case. The system is, however, Israeli, not English or American.

Juries are not used in Israeli trials. Cases are heard by a single judge or, in major cases (including cases that can result in long-term imprisonment or the death penalty), a panel of three judges. When a panel of judges is used, decision is by majority vote.

The few crimes in Israel that carry the death penalty—only acts of genocide and specific war crimes—must be tried with a member of the Israeli Supreme Court presiding. Justice Moshe Landau would preside over the Eichmann trial, along with Benjamin Halevy, president of the Jerusalem district court, and Yitzhak Raveh, a member of the Tel Aviv district court. All three were born and educated in Germany. All had come to Palestine at the very beginning of the Nazi era, so none had directly experienced the Holocaust.

Televising the Trial

The first major ruling in the case actually occurred about a month before the trial began. The Eichmann trial was the first trial in history to be televised. The judges gave permission, over the objections of Eichmann's attorney, for the trial to be filmed. The technology did

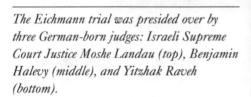

The Eichmann trial was presided over by three German-born judges: Israeli Supreme Court Justice Moshe Landau (top), Benjamin Halevy (middle), and Yitzhak Raveh (bottom).

TELEVISING THE PROCEEDINGS

Eichmann's counsel, Robert Servatius, objected to film recording of the trial, realizing its potential for portraying his client in the worst possible light. This excerpt from the transcripts of the proceedings outlines his argument and the judges' counterargument.

Dr. Servatius, Counsel for the Defence, has strongly opposed the request of the Attorney General. His main arguments are the following:

(a) The knowledge that the proceedings are being recorded for television and cinema may induce the witnesses not to give their evidence truthfully, both because they may be afraid of persons outside the courtroom who may be watching their televised evidence and because of a desire to playact before a world-wide audience.

(b) The television broadcasts are apt to lead to a distorted presentation of the proceedings, e.g., by omitting the arguments of the Defence.

Alternatively, Dr. Servatius has requested the Court to make its consent conditional upon the Capital Cities Broadcasting Corporation undertaking that in disseminating the pictures and recordings it will give an objective presentation of the proceedings. . . .

As to the accuracy of the publication, there can be no doubt that direct visual and sound recording in the manner intended will render the proceedings in courtroom with complete faithfulness. . . . We therefore hold that in view of the aforesaid fundamental considerations—widest possible publication, for the benefit of every person desiring to be informed, and exposure of the court to the judgement of the public—a television broadcast of what happens in the courtroom is not only not objectionable, but serves important interests of justice, and that we must not withhold the approval of the Court from this method merely because it constitutes an innovation.

not exist for the immediate, live coverage possible today, so the trial was filmed by a single television network which then made copies available to all other interested networks and stations. In the United States, for example, ABC presented a weekly one-hour summary. ABC's New York affiliate offered a half-hour summary each evening. Filming was justified as important to the educational function of the trial, enabling people to see as well as

Observers monitor television coverage of the Eichmann trial, the first in history to be televised. The man on the right has a concentration camp number tattooed on his forearm.

read about what was happening. However, the judges specifically ordered that filming not interfere with normal, proper trial procedure.

Opening Motions

Trials deal with legal matters before they deal with questions of fact and with the primary question of the defendant's guilt or innocence. Frequently, a trial begins with motions by the defense to throw out all or part of the prosecution's case. The defense may question the court's jurisdiction, whether or not the court has a right to try the defendant. If the court has no right to try the defendant, the case would end with the defendant's release or transfer to a court that does have jurisdiction over the case. Legal motions can be tedious, and the Eichmann trial was no exception. However,

Israel's right to try Eichmann was controversial, and the issue generated considerable interest at the outset.

Presenting the Charges

Before these legal issues could be settled, Eichmann was formally identified and the charges against him were read. He was charged with fifteen counts under Sections 1 and 3 of the Nazis and Nazi Collaborators (Punishment) Law of 1950. The first count dealt with the murder of 6 million Jews, the ultimate result of the final solution. The second count charged Eichmann with placing them, before they were killed, in conditions designed to bring about their physical destruction. Count three accused Eichmann of causing his Jewish victims grave physical and mental harm; count four with devising measures for preventing Jewish childbirth, including sterilization; count five with enslaving, starving, and deporting the Jews. The sixth count in the indictment charged Eichmann with general persecution of Jews on national, racial, religious, and political grounds. Count seven dealt with appropriating Jewish property by means of compulsion, robbery, terror, and violence. Count eight stated that these acts were all, under Israeli law, punishable war crimes.

THE QUESTION OF EX POST FACTO LAW

Ex post facto laws make illegal and are designed to punish acts committed before the law was passed. Ex post facto laws are unconstitutional in the United States, and banned in other democracies. The issue came up in the debate over Israel's legal right to try Eichmann. American legal expert Milton Katz responded in the Israelis' defense in a 1961 *New Jersey Law Journal*. His comments are reprinted in the American Jewish Committee's "The Eichmann Case: Moral and Legal Arguments."

> The theory of non-retroactive statutes, *ex post facto* laws and all the rest, is that you have no right to make criminal something which wasn't criminal when the man committed it. Well, when Eichmann committed his acts, they were in violation of well established doctrines of international law as they then stood. And it would be very hard, I think, to suggest that Eichmann would be surprised to learn that murdering six million people would not be thought by other people to be criminal.

Counts nine, ten, eleven, and twelve dealt with extermination of non-Jews. Eichmann was accused of helping deport 500,000 Poles, 14,000 Slovenes, and thousands of Gypsies, as well as 100 Czech children from the village of Lidice, Czechoslovakia. The last three counts dealt with membership in organizations declared criminal at the Nuremberg trials, including the SS. Each of the first twelve charges carried the death penalty as the maximum punishment.

The Judges' Objectivity Is Questioned

Eichmann was asked to plead guilty or innocent to the charges. At this point, however, his lawyer, Robert Servatius, moved to present his arguments against the trial's continuance. For forty-five minutes during the first session Servatius presented his major arguments verbally, then submitted a lengthy written brief.

Servatius's arguments first questioned the judges' objectivity. All Jews were affected by the Holocaust, Servatius argued, so Jewish judges could not avoid bias. "The fear of prejudice exists, therefore, against all the judges in equal measure," Servatius said. "There are reasons which arise in general from the very material of the proceedings." [38] The defense was objecting not to any of the three judges in particular, but to all Jewish judges.

Servatius also objected to what he called political influence on the trial, and to the "influence of the world political press, which has already condemned the Accused without hearing him. This political interest

Servatius argued that the trial should not proceed because it was impossible for the Jewish judges to be fair and objective.

which is the motivating cause of this trial, is capable of having substantial influence on the judges." [39]

Attacking Israel's Right to Try Eichmann

The defense attorney then attacked the Israeli law under which Eichmann was being tried, the Nazis and Nazi Collaborators (Punishment) Law. Servatius claimed this law violated international law. Under this law, he said, a man could be tried for deeds committed outside Israeli territory and before Israel became an independent state. Servatius claimed that the 1950 law made people accountable not only for acts committed before the law was passed, but for acts considered legal under the system prevailing when they were committed.

Servatius went on to argue that Eichmann's actions were not personal, but acts of state. Writing about the Eichmann trial, legal scholar Michael Patrick Murray defines acts of state as

> any act accomplished by an agent of the state, whether he be the head of state or subordinate thereto, within the scope of his agency, should be considered solely an act of the state for which the state alone is responsible. [40]

The Nazis and Nazi Collaborator (Punishment) Law smacked of revenge, according to the defense counsel. Servatius asserted that the accused could not make amends for the actions of his state.

Related to the acts of state defense was the "following orders" defense, which Servatius mentioned in these initial arguments. Servatius argued that Eichmann's actions were allegedly in response to the orders of and under the supervision of his superiors in the chain of command. He owed them his unquestioned allegiance. The same defense arose, and was rejected, at the Nuremberg trials, and has since become known as the "Nuremberg defense." Yet this would be the central theme of Eichmann's formal defense later in the trial.

Servatius finally raised the issue of Eichmann's kidnapping. According to Servatius, proof of this abduction, for which he wanted to call two participants as witnesses, would deprive the

Israeli court of jurisdiction over a defendant "illegally" brought before the court.

Hausner Plans His Response

The brief Servatius submitted outlining his objections presented Hausner with a problem. Israeli procedure called for oral arguments, while German procedure favored the use of written briefs. The prosecution had agreed to let Servatius follow German procedure. Hausner, though tempted to ask for a similar exception for the prosecution, decided to follow Israeli procedure. Hausner's reply would take four sessions, lasting through the second day of the trial.

At the end of the first day of the trial, Hausner had not finished his reply to Servatius's arguments. A senior government official friend cautioned him not to prolong the argument on strategic grounds:

> Servatius spoke for three-quarters of an hour. People did not hear his written brief, and they will think his arguments are very strong if they need so long a reply. Besides, there are over five hundred journalists and observers here from abroad. . . . They are bored with the legal debate; think of what they will write home.[41]

Hausner agreed with his friend but felt he had no choice but to proceed with his full oral argument, to choose legal procedure over drama.

Hausner's Response

Hausner first responded to the fair trial issue. He argued that "a judge can be just, although he cannot be expected to be impartial toward crime." He added that "If there was a man in the world 'neutral' toward genocide, it was he who should be disqualified as a judge."[42] Hausner later pointed out that Servatius had wanted Eichmann tried in Germany. It was strange, Hausner wrote, that judges should be disqualified for being fellow nationals of the victims, but not for being fellow nationals of the accused.

On the abduction issue, Hausner cited a long series of American and British decisions that considered irrelevant how a defendant came before a court. Once the defendant is physically present, the court will proceed with the trial. Abduction across borders may be a political issue between two nations (as it was between Israel and Argentina), but not an issue for the courts. Among his examples, Hausner cited a 1952 U.S. Supreme Court decision that stated, "This court has never departed from the rule . . . that the power of a Court to try a person for crime is not impaired by the fact that he has been brought within the Court's jurisdiction by reason of a forcible abduction." [43]

Territorial Limits on Jurisdiction

Hausner then addressed the question of territorial limits on jurisdiction. Many countries, Hausner pointed out, claim jurisdiction over crimes against their nationals regardless of where they are committed. He went further, pointing out that some crimes are considered to strike at the welfare of humanity at large; that is, crimes against humanity. Any country not only could try, but is obliged to try these crimes. Any country could claim this right, and accept this responsibility, even if the crime was committed before the country existed. Furthermore Israel may not have existed during World War II but it was the "successor state" to the Jewish community in Palestine, which had been recognized since 1917.

As a result of active Jewish participation on the side of the Allies in World War II, Israel was recognized as a cobelligerent and had been invited in 1954 to formally terminate the state of war with West Germany. Finally, no other country affected by Eichmann's alleged crimes or connected with Eichmann, including Argentina, had formally filed for his extradition. According to the prosecution, it was not only Israel's right, but Israel's responsibility to try Eichmann.

Hausner was the first to raise the statute of limitations issue (perhaps inspiring Servatius to do so at the end of the trial) as a side issue to that of territorial limits on jurisdiction. A statute of limitation is a time limit after which a person can no longer be prosecuted for a particular act. Hausner argued that no country had formally requested Eichmann's extradition. Argentina had demanded his return after the kidnapping became public, but the matter was dropped when the formal Israeli apology for the kidnapping settled the issue. Argentina had a statute of limitations of fifteen years for war crimes, and thus would have refused a request for extradition after its expiration. No other country had claimed jurisdiction, so the choice was between trying Eichmann in Israel or letting him go.

Rejecting Dismissal

Hausner also addressed Servatius's complaint about the Nazis and Nazi Collaborator (Punishment) Law. Hausner pointed out

EXTENDING THE STATUTE OF LIMITATIONS

In the mid-1960s, the West German government debated the question of a statute of limitations for the prosecution of Nazi war crimes. German philosopher Karl Jaspers, as quoted in Azriel Eisenberg's *Witness to the Holocaust*, came out strongly against such limitations. Such statues were never passed.

I doubt if there has ever been this crime in its unique sense before. I know of no instance. . . . I do think we must recognize that we are here dealing with an essentially unprecedented crime before we can make a judgement on the question of the Statute of Limitations. The answer to this question will become quite obvious if we have a clear view of four closely connected questions. The first one is this: What kind of crime? Administrative mass murder, a crime without precedent in history. The crime presupposed a new kind of state— the criminal state. The second question: According to what law is a judgement made? According to international law, the law that binds all men together. The third question: What is the legitimate instrument for the application of this law? As long as humanity does not have the proper legal institution for handling it, the proper authority are the courts of those states that recognize the validity of international law in their own jurisprudence. The fourth question is this: What punishment? The punishment in keeping with this unique crime against humanity is capital punishment, an exceptional punishment reinstated in this exceptional case even after its abolition. These questions have not been cleared up to this day.

that at the Nuremberg trials (1945–1949), defense counsel had protested that the acts being tried were legal at the time they were committed. Counsel had claimed that the acts could not be made illegal retroactively by laws passed after the acts were carried out. In rejecting the "retroactive law" defense, the various Nuremberg trial judges ruled that the defendants were acting "not only in defiance of well-established principles of International Law, but in complete disregard of the elementary dictates of humanity." [44] A decision at one of the later Nuremberg trials ruled that the fundamental crime with which most defendants were charged was murder, and that murder has always been considered a crime. Hausner reemphasized this point.

Hausner also pointed out that "following orders" was not a blanket defense that would absolve an individual of the need to judge right from wrong. He added that "Even under the law applicable under the Nazis it was no defense to a criminal charge for a subordinate to claim 'superior orders' if according to his idea and concepts the act enjoined upon him was wrongful." [45] When Justice Landau, the presiding judge, asked for clarification of "ideas and concepts," Hausner offered to let Eichmann come forward and prove that the Holocaust was not a wrongful act.

The Judges Decide

Servatius briefly responded to Hausner on April 16, the fifth session of the trial. Basically he reiterated the arguments presented in his oral and written statements.

The judges announced their decision the next day. They rejected all of Servatius's objections. The judges ruled that Israel had jurisdiction over Eichmann, that the method by which he was brought to the court was irrelevant, that any limits on extradition did not matter since Eichmann was not extradited. Additionally, his kidnapping was an offense only to Argentina, and that matter had been settled.

Addressing the question of their objectivity, the judges declared that they would be able to put their personal feelings aside. They would be able to follow the principle, as they declared in their judgment, that every man is deemed to be innocent and that his case must be tried only on the basis of evidence brought before the Court. Those charged with the task of judging are professional judges accustomed to weighing evidence and they will be carrying out their task under the critical gaze of the public.[46]

At the same session, Eichmann pled to all counts "not guilty in the sense of the indictment." No one asked in what sense he may have been guilty.

A few minutes later, Hausner arose to make his opening statement.

Opening Statement

Gideon Hausner was forty-six at the time Eichmann's trial began. He came to Palestine with his family at age twelve, well before the Holocaust. Hausner never seemed to doubt his ability to handle the legal aspects of the trial. However, while preparing for the trial, he felt some apprehension about whether, as someone with no direct experience of the Holocaust, he could speak for the victims. As part of his research for the trial, Hausner spent an evening with Yitzhak and Zivia Zuckerman, surviving leaders of the 1943 Warsaw ghetto revolt, the most famous (but failed) Jewish rebellion against the Nazis. After talking for several hours, there was silence. Then Zivia Zuckerman remarked, "You know, you talk as if you were there with us." [47] Hausner had educated himself on the Holocaust, as well as anyone could, and now felt ready to educate others.

Several days into the trial, Hausner rose to begin his case:

> When I stand before you here, Judges of Israel, to lead the Prosecution of Adolf Eichmann, I am not standing alone. With me are six million accusers. But they cannot rise to their feet and point an accusing finger towards him who sits in the dock and cry: "I accuse." For their ashes are piled up on the hills of Auschwitz and the fields of Treblinka, and are strewn in the forests of Poland. Their graves are scattered throughout the length

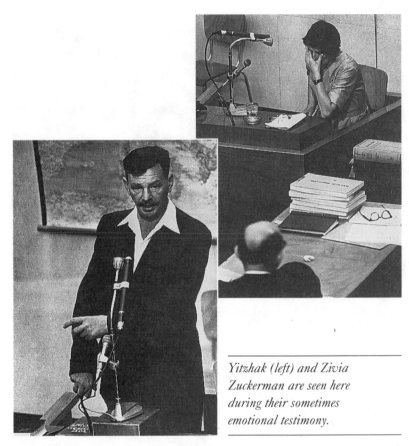

*Yitzhak (left) and Zivia
Zuckerman are seen here
during their sometimes
emotional testimony.*

and breadth of Europe. Their blood cries out, but their voice is not heard. Therefore I will be their spokesman and in their name will I unfold the awesome indictment.

The history of the Jewish people is steeped in suffering and tears. . . . Yet never, down in the entire blood-stained road travelled by this people, never since the first days of its nationhood, has any man arisen who succeeded in dealing it such grievous blows as did Hitler's iniquitous regime, and Adolf Eichmann as its executive arm for the extermination of the Jewish People. In all human history there is no other example of a man against whom it would be possible to draw up such a bill of indictment as has been read here.[48]

A survivor of Buchenwald concentration camp points to a former tormentor in 1945. Sixteen years later, Gideon Hausner would be the spokesman for those who did not survive the atrocities of Eichmann and the Nazi regime.

Outlining the Prosecution's Case

Hausner used his opening statement to survey the crimes of which Eichmann was accused. After the strong opening, he noted that murder has been with humanity since the biblical Cain killed Abel.

> But we have had to wait until this twentieth century to witness with our own eyes a new kind of murder: not the result of the momentary ebullition of passion or the darkening of the soul, but of a calculated decision and painstaking planning; not through the evil design of an individual, but through a mighty criminal conspiracy involving thousands; not against one victim whom an assassin may have decided to destroy, but against an entire nation.

> In this trial, we shall also encounter a new kind of killer, the kind that exercises his bloody craft behind a desk.[49]

Hausner then briefly sketched Eichmann's career. He discussed the efficiency of the Holocaust, emphasizing the results of Eichmann's administrative handiwork. He told of the continual deportation and then elimination of Jews in all parts of Europe, ending with the rushed efforts to send Hungary's Jews to death camps in the last days of the war. Hausner stressed the zealousness with which Eichmann pursued the rounding up of Hungarian Jews even though the war was clearly at an end. In his book on the trial, Hausner described this act as "Eichmann's feverish attempt to finish off his task." [50]

Hausner then moved back in time to describe prewar European Jewry, in effect setting the scene of the crime. He spoke of the vibrant and prospering communities of Jews that would be destroyed by Nazi anti-Semitism. The last section of the address reviewed the charges and outlined the evidence the prosecution intended to produce.

Hungarian Jews are loaded aboard a train bound for Auschwitz in 1944. In what Hausner described as a "feverish attempt to finish off his task," Eichmann continued rounding up Jews for extermination even as the war was ending.

DIFFICULT CONDITIONS?

In *Eichmann Interrogated,* edited by Jochen von Lang, Israeli police captain Avner W. Less describes the conditions under which Eichmann was confined.

Eichmann's cell, measuring roughly ten by thirteen feet, contained only a cot, a table, and a chair. The electric light was left on all night. Every day he cleaned his cell and the adjoining toilet and shower room unaided. He did these chores with thoroughness and dedication. A guard sat in the room with him day and night, and outside the cell door sat a second guard, who watched the one in the cell through a peephole, to make sure there was no contact between him and Eichmann. The second guard was in a kind of vestibule, outside the door of which a third guard kept constant watch on him.

These security measures were not designed to prevent Eichmann from attacking the guard in his cell so much as to prevent him from committing suicide. That was our greatest fear; if he had succeeded in committing suicide, no one anywhere in the world would have believed it. That is why we guarded him like the apple of our eye. During the first weeks, when the electric light disturbed his sleep,

Eichmann is given a physical examination in his cell under the careful scrutiny of a security guard.

he would pull his woolen blanket over his head, whereupon the guard would pull it back to make sure Eichmann was not trying to kill himself under the blanket. Twice a day he was examined from head to toe by our police physician.

Hausner ended his opening statement by attesting to the ironic character of a legal trial, in a Jewish courtroom, deciding the fate of the man who had decided the fate of 6 million Jews:

Adolf Eichmann will enjoy a privilege he did not accord to even a single one of his victims. He will be able to defend himself before the court. His fate will be decided according to the law and the evidence, with the burden of proof resting upon the prosecution.

And the judges of Israel will pronounce true and righteous judgement.[51]

Hausner's speech had taken eight hours to deliver, and stretched over three sessions. With the dramatic ending to this opening statement, Hausner began to present his evidence.

Chapter 4

The Prosecution
Presents Its Case

CHIEF PROSECUTOR GIDEON HAUSNER had called Eichmann a "desk murderer" in his opening address. Prosecuting a desk murderer, one who gave the orders but did not actually do the killing, presented problems. Witnesses were able to describe the crimes that took place, but few had actually seen Eichmann, a man who stayed in the background. The prosecution had to establish that the horrors the Jews faced were a result of his efficient management skills. Without being able to force Eichmann to testify as part of their case, Hausner and his team had to have witnesses describe the horrors of the Holocaust and then prove through documents that Eichmann had helped cause those horrors.

Prosecution Tactics

Hausner began his case by calling witnesses to describe the specific crimes they had witnessed and/or endured. The prosecution eventually called 112 witnesses, a few of whom were legal or historical experts, called to provide background in their field of expertise. Most, however, were Holocaust survivors. The prosecution provided documents to connect Eichmann to the crimes the witnesses described. Hausner hoped that by combining emotional eyewitness accounts with the written records the prosecution's case would offer a dramatic educational experience for Israel and the world. Hausner felt it would also meet the legal need to conclusively prove Eichmann's guilt.

Hausner (standing to address the court at left) called a total of 112 witnesses, most of whom were Holocaust survivors. The judges challenged the pertinence of some of their testimonies.

Connecting witnesses to Eichmann was often difficult. Some observers thought that the prosecution's method was saying more about the horrors of the Holocaust than about Eichmann's complicity. The judges sometimes showed impatience with Hausner's approach, questioning the relevance of particular testimony to Eichmann's guilt.

However, Hausner did try to make the parade of witness testimony relevant. Hausner contended, and presented documents designed to prove, that when witnesses spoke of the inhuman conditions of life in the ghetto, Eichmann had played a significant role in corralling them there. When survivors told harrowing stories of being crammed into boxcars that were not unloaded until they reached the death camps, Hausner attested that it was Eichmann who made sure the trains ran. The prosecution sought to prove that, toward the end of the war, Eichmann made sure there were enough trains designated to carry this human cargo, even at the expense of the German war effort. Hausner

Professor Salo Baron (at the podium), an expert on European Jewry, was called to the witness stand by Hausner (standing at right) to describe the thriving European Jewish culture that existed prior to the war and how the Nazis systematically destroyed that culture.

called witnesses to speak of death marches ordered by Eichmann once railroad lines had been destroyed by Allied bombing. Because these marches had no specified destination they served no purpose but to kill Jews through exhaustion and exposure. Hausner made sure that his audience understood that it was Eichmann who had ordered such cruel and inhuman acts.

Initial Witnesses to Lay Groundwork

Hausner's first witness was a senior Israeli police officer who introduced the lengthy transcript of Eichmann's interrogation by the police. The entire document was prosecution evidence; Hausner wanted to be able to refer to particular parts during his case.

Hausner then called an expert on European Jewry, Professor Salo Baron of New York City's Columbia University. Baron described the European Jewish world that Eichmann had played so important a role in destroying. He described the thriving Jewish culture that existed in the 1930s, and went on to detail the Nazis' systematic destruction of that culture. Baron described the world Eichmann found and the shards he left behind.

The Night of Broken Glass

With the groundwork for the Holocaust laid, Hausner offered testimony from Jews who had suffered at the hands of the Nazis. Hausner's next witness was Zyndel Schmeul Grynszpan, a Polish Jew living in Germany in 1938. Grynszpan was among twelve thousand non-German Jews expelled from Germany in October of 1938. Though Eichmann was not involved in this particular deportation, it began the chain of events leading to Eichmann being called to Berlin and given increasing responsibility over Jewish affairs.

Grynszpan's teenage son, Herszel, was visiting his uncle in Paris while his parents were deported from Germany. When Herszel learned of his family's plight, he decided to take revenge. He went to the German embassy in Paris, and shot the first German

Zyndel Schmeul Grynszpan (left) testifies about how the Nazis made his family suffer. After the Nazis expelled Grynszpan from Germany in 1938, his son, Herszel, sought revenge by killing a diplomat at the German embassy in Paris.

Herszel Grynspan's murder of a German diplomat set off Kristallnacht, a night of mass destruction, murder, and arrests. Here, Germans pass by the broken shop window of a Jewish-owned business that was destroyed during Kristallnacht.

diplomat he saw. The diplomat's death provoked the November 9, 1938, orgy of destruction organized by Reinhard Heydrich, head of the RSHA (the German security service), known as Kristallnacht, the Night of Broken Glass. Descriptions of wholesale destruction of Jewish property, murder, and mass arrests were entered into evidence by the prosecution.

Hausner then introduced into evidence the verbatim transcript of a German conference held not long after Kristallnacht. Hermann Goering, in charge of the German economy as well as of the German air force, summoned a high-level ministerial meeting to discuss ways to exclude the Jews from the German economy. Reinhard Heydrich attended the meeting and recommended that a central office of emigration be established in Germany to expel the Jews from the country, not just the economy. Heydrich said that this office would be similar to the highly effective office already operating in Austria. Goering objected to the cost, and Heydrich responded that the Austrian Jews were being made to pay for their own deportation.

Heydrich's detailed explanation of the Austrian system impressed the others at the conference, and his suggestion was accepted. Heydrich suggested that the head of the Austrian office, the man responsible for Austria's efficient system of deportation, could head the expanded Berlin-based office. The man was Adolf Eichmann.

The Next Step

The next step in the escalating persecution of the Jews, as presented by Hausner, arose after the German invasion of Poland and the start of World War II in September 1939. The rapid German advance brought them into contact with many of the Jews

Reinhard Heydrich (left) and Hermann Goering (right) were instrumental in forming the office that Eichmann headed during the war.

they had expelled from Austria and Germany. There were also about 3 million native Polish Jews. Expulsion of so large a group from German-controlled territory was no longer feasible. The next step, therefore, was forcing the Jews into concentrated areas (usually in cities) called ghettos. In effect this was a transition phase, containing the Jews until a more permanent solution could be found.

Heydrich accepted the responsibility of forming these ghettos, but he assigned the actual organizing to Eichmann. Documentary evidence at the trial indicated that a new office within the RSHA, IV-D-4, was created for Eichmann. Eichmann would remain in charge of this subsection until the end of the war, though its role would change, and Eichmann would undertake special assignments such as helping plan the extermination chambers at the largest Nazi death camp, Auschwitz.

The Dangers of Resistance

Hausner's chronology of the Holocaust moved on to the creation of the most famous ghetto, that in Warsaw, the capital of Poland. Hausner presented the terrible conditions under which Polish Jews had to live. He also wanted to show what happened to Jews who offered resistance to the Nazis or their henchmen. Resistance was dangerous, and not just for active participants. The Germans skillfully used terror to enforce collective responsibility for individual acts. One example was given by Warsaw ghetto survivor Zivia Lubetkin Zuckerman, the same woman who earlier told Hausner "you sound like you were there":

> In the early days of the ghetto a Polish policeman [working for the Nazis] was looking for a certain Jew to take vengeance upon him, to arrest him. The Jew drew a pistol and killed the Polish policeman. As retribution for this, the Germans, the following morning, entered [a courtyard], removed 50 Jews from among those living in this courtyard and from those who happened to be there by chance. They were taken away, and didn't return to their families.[52]

Hungry residents of the Warsaw Ghetto gather in the marketplace. A survivor of the ghetto testified about the appalling living conditions and of the deadly consequences that occurred when residents tried to resist their Nazi captors.

Many found unclear the connection between Eichmann and such tales of retribution. Hausner, however, was trying to emphasize to young Israelis, and to the world at large, that some Jews did resist their Nazi captors. He sought to educate his audience about the Holocaust as well as to assign blame to Eichmann. Yet for some critics these digressions were obviously irrelevant to the conviction.

Even the judges did not always see the relevance of some of the witnesses. They felt that the educational aims of Hausner's case were sometimes superseding legal matters. Presiding judge Moshe Landau raised this issue with Hausner at the start of Session 25 (May 3, 1961) just before a Warsaw ghetto survivor began to testify:

We are not [supposed to be] presenting a picture [of the Holocaust] here. If the picture is portrayed incidentally in the course of the trial—well and good; but we have an indictment and this indictment constitutes a framework for the trial. . . . It is along these lines that the witness, too, must be questioned.[53]

Hausner found it particularly difficult to enter testimony on resistance into evidence, as one trial observer noted, simply because "Legally, the testimony of these witnesses was immaterial."[54] Hausner argued that the behavior of victims was relevant to a crime, and that those who died resisting are just as much murder victims as those who did not resist. Hausner chose, however, to shorten the amount of testimony. He did not want to risk a judicial decision against some of the oral evidence, fearing that in the eyes of the world it would taint all the evidence.

Much of the testimony, however, came from witnesses who could not directly implicate Eichmann. It was up to the prosecution to show through documentary evidence that Eichmann had a hand in the horrors that the witnesses described. Some critics were skeptical of this method, especially when witnesses were called to speak about atrocities that had not been well documented. This lack of connecting evidence, however, did not lessen the impact of the testimony on those who watched the trial.

A Dramatic Tale

Perhaps the most moving testimony came from Rivka Yoselewska, a Polish Jew who described the activities of the Einsatzgruppen, military units that followed the German army as it progressed through conquered territories. Their mission was to round up and eliminate any Jews they came across. Yoselewska was allowed to speak though the prosecution could show only that Eichmann had issued orders to the Einsatzgruppen on rare occasions. The audience was riveted, however, as Yoselewska recalled the autumn of 1941, when the Einsatzgruppen came to her town, herded the Jews to a spot two miles away and there systematically shot their victims at the edge of a large pit:

> When we [the witness, her young daughter, her parents, siblings, relatives, and other Jews] arrived at this place, we saw naked people standing there already. . . . To get

away was impossible. I was curious to see whether anybody was below that hill where the people had to stand and I made a quick turn. I saw three or four rows, twelve people already killed. . . .

Some of the younger ones tried to run away. They hardly managed a few steps, they were caught and shot. Then came our turn. It was difficult to hold the children, they were shaking. We took turns. Parents took the children, took other people's children. This was to help us get through it all; to get it over with and not see the children suffer. . . .

We were lined up in fours. We stood there naked. [Her parents and grandmother were shot.] Then my turn came. My younger sister also. She had suffered so much in the ghetto, and yet at the last moment she wanted to stay alive, and begged the German to let her live. She was standing there naked holding on to her girl friend. So he looked at her and shot them both. . . . My older sister was next. Then he got ready to shoot me. . . .

Somewhere in Poland, Jewish women and children are lined up for their execution after being ordered to undress. The courtroom was riveted by shocking descriptions of numerous atrocities such as this in Nazi-held lands.

We [she was clutching her daughter] stood there facing the ditch. I turned my head. He asked, "Whom do I shoot first?" I didn't answer. He tore the child away from me. I heard her last cry and he shot her. Then he got ready to kill me, grabbed my hair and turned my head about. I remained standing and heard a shot but I didn't move. He turned me around, loaded his pistol, so that I could see what he was doing. Then he again turned me around and shot me. I fell down. . . .

[After falling into the pit] I could move and felt I was alive and tried to get up. . . . I felt I was going to suffocate. . . . I felt that somehow I was crawling upwards. As I climbed up, people grabbed me, hit me, dragged me downwards, but I pulled myself upwards with the last bit of strength. When I reached the top I looked around but I couldn't recognize the place. Corpses strewn all over. . . . You could hear people moaning in their death

An executioner finishes off the last of his victims. One of the most compelling testimonies of the trial come from a woman who survived such an ordeal.

agony. Some children were running around naked and screaming "Mama, Papa." I couldn't get up.[55]

The Germans had left. The witness was "naked and covered with blood," from her own head wound and, primarily, from the blood of other victims. She got up and went over to a group of children, to see if her daughter was among them, but her daughter was not there. She saw two other women, and with them pulled a fourth woman out of a pile of bodies. A day or so later the Germans came back, with some local non-Jews. The locals were forced to pile the bodies in one place. The children who were still there were shot, as was the young woman the witness had rescued. There is no mention of what happened to the other two women. Yoselewska, the witness, sat dazed near the graves but was ignored by the Germans:

> When I saw they were done I dragged myself over to the grave and wanted to jump in. I thought the grave would open up and let me fall inside alive. I envied everyone for whom it was already over, while I was still alive. Where should I go? What should I do? Blood was spouting. Nowadays, when I pass a water fountain I can still see the blood spouting from the grave. The earth rose and heaved. I sat there on the grave and tried to dig my way in with my hands. I continued digging as hard as I could. The earth didn't open up. I shouted to Mother and Father, why was I left alive? What did I do to deserve this? Where shall I go? To whom can I turn? I have nobody. I saw everything; I saw everybody killed. No one answered. I remained sprawled on the grave three days and three nights.[56]

She left the grave after some cattle herders saw her, but stayed nearby. She was finally rescued by a Polish peasant who gave her food and clothing. Yoselewska joined a group of Jewish partisans in the forest, and was able to survive the war.

Hausner asked the witness one final question. "And now you are married and you have two children?" "Yes,"[57] the witness responded.

According to Hausner, "Her story shattered the court-room."[58] Eichmann's defense attorney announced that he had no questions for Yoselewska. Servatius chose not to cross-examine most witnesses since his strategy was not to deny what happened, just to deny Eichmann's role. In fact, Eichmann may have had no connection to Yoselewska's tale, but Hausner made it clear that the Einsatzgruppen to which Eichmann did issue orders would have performed similar duties.

The Final Solution

Heinrich Himmler and other Nazi leaders considered the face-to-face shooting of victims to be too hard emotionally on most members of the Einsatzgruppen. They sought another method, faster and less of a strain on the troops. In January 1942 they devised the "final solution," the organized mass murder of Jews in specially designed death camps. No specific written order from Adolf Hitler has been found to authorize this organized mass murder, though his verbal approval would have been necessary.

In 1941, before the facilities at the death camps were put into operation, Eichmann went to Auschwitz to talk with the camp's commander, Rudolf Hoess. Eichmann and Hoess discussed the use of gas to kill Jews. Eichmann even helped plan the layout of the gas chambers and was part of the decision to use a form of cyanide called Zyklon B as the principal poison. Hoess testified about Eichmann's role at the major war crimes trial in Nuremberg. Hoess was hanged for his war crimes two years after the war, so he could not be called at Eichmann's trial. Yet Hoess had written incriminating memoirs which were introduced into evidence at Eichmann's trial.

Eichmann's name appears often in Hoess's memoirs. Eichmann was the man, according to Hoess, who sent him Jews to kill and kept detailed records of the exterminations. Eichmann was also the one who encouraged Hoess to continue his extermination when Hoess became bothered by what he was doing. Hoess wrote that Eichmann

> was totally obsessed with the idea of destroying every
> Jew he could get his hands on. Ice cold and without

During the Nuremberg war crimes trials, Auschwitz commander Rudolf Hoess (center) stated that Eichmann was instrumental in designing and implementing the use of gas chambers as a method of mass murder.

mercy, we had to carry out this annihilation as quickly as possible. Any compromise, even the smallest, would bitterly avenge itself later on.

Faced with such grim determination I had to bury all my human inhibitions as deeply as possible. In fact, I have to confess openly that after such conversations with Eichmann these human emotions seemed almost like treason against [Hitler].[59]

In response to a question from Hausner, attempting to verify Hoess's statements, psychologist G. M. Gilbert (who had spoken at length with Hoess and also testified at Nuremberg)

A POOR DECEPTION

The issue of awareness of Nazi genocide was brought up at Eichmann's trial. William Shirer quotes Rudolf Hoess, commandant of the main Nazi death camp, Auschwitz, in *The Rise and Fall of the Third Reich.*

> Still another improvement we made over Treblinka was that at Treblinka the victims almost always knew that they were to be exterminated, while at Auschwitz we endeavored to fool the victims into thinking that they were to go through a delousing process. Of course, frequently they realized our true intentions and sometimes we had riots and difficulties. Very frequently women would hide their children under the clothes but of course when we found them we would send the children in to be exterminated.

> We were required to carry out these exterminations in secrecy, but of course the foul and nauseating stench from the continuous burning of bodies permeated the entire area and all of the people living in the surrounding communities knew that exterminations were going on at Auschwitz.

testified that Hoess was "a man who was just automatically telling the facts as he knew them . . . without any attempt to share blame, or to attempt defense or anything." [60] Hausner felt he had successfully connected Eichmann to the creation of the machines of death; now he turned to Eichmann's role as the administrator who fed those machines.

Death Camp Operation

Documents were presented to connect Eichmann to the sending of Jews to the death camps, particularly to the deportation of Jews from western and southern Europe, Germany, Austria, and Hungary. Hausner called witnesses to describe how the death camps implemented the assembly-line murder of human beings. Hausner argued that this was the end result of Eichmann's documented efforts. Other witnesses described in detail the usual procedures for mass murder at Auschwitz and the other five major German death camps. Upon arrival, people selected for death were marched off to places to undress. They were usually informed they would be taking showers for health purposes. Their clothing was stacked neatly. Once they had been crowded into the gas chamber itself, made to look like a shower room, the doors were locked. Crystals of Zyklon B were dropped in through openings in the ceiling, releasing hydrogen cyanide gas. All the people were soon unconscious and dead within fifteen to twenty minutes.

The bodies were removed by Jewish prisoners detailed for that purpose. Gold teeth were extracted and women's hair cut, both to be shipped back to Germany. The bodies were burned in special crematoria (ovens) designed for that purpose. Near the end of the war, bodies were sometimes just dumped in pits.

German concentration camp workers (left) hold canisters of Zyklon B, the poison used to kill Jews in the gas chambers. After being put to death, the victims were removed by Jewish prisoners who cut women's hair and extracted gold teeth from the corpses, which were then cremated in special ovens (below).

Some occasions were cited where the human ashes, usually also buried, were used to cover ice-coated walkways in the winter. The German guards did not want to slip and injure themselves.

All of the analytic descriptions of the methods of killing made Hausner feel as though the testimony was so abstract that it ran the risk of being unimaginable. To compensate Hausner ended this portion of the testimony with visual evidence of the horrors so vividly described. He showed a film combining captured German films with those taken when the camps were liberated. It clearly brought the atrocities into focus and documented the reality of the witnesses' testimonies.

The film was not the end of the prosecution's case. Hausner wanted to end on a more positive note, and so introduced testimony from Jewish partisans who struggled against the Nazis. Since the link between Eichmann's crimes and partisan activity

At the end of the war, the liberators of this Nazi death camp encountered the gruesome sight of thousands of rotting corpses. Hausner added a moving visual component to the trial by showing a film that contained German footage of the camps during the war as well as images taken after they were liberated.

THE WARSAW GHETTO UPRISING

The following is an excerpt from the Eichmann trial testimony of Zivia Lubetkin Zuckerman, one of the surviving leaders of the Warsaw ghetto revolt.

When the day dawned [April 18, 1943] . . . I saw the thousands of Germans who were surrounding the ghetto—with machine guns, with cannon—and thousands of them, with their weapons, as if they were going to the Russian front. And there we stood opposite them—some twenty young men and women. What were our weapons? Each one had a revolver, each one had a hand grenade; the entire unit had two rifles, and in addition we had homemade bombs, primitive ones. . . . It was very strange to see that some Jewish boys and girls, confronting this enormous enemy with all his weapons, were joyful and merry. . . .We knew that our end had come. We knew beforehand that they would defeat us, but we also knew that they would pay a heavy price for our lives. . . . It is difficult to describe, and there will surely be many who do not believe it, that when the Germans came near the foot of one of our strongholds and passed by in formation, and we threw the bombs and the hand-grenades, and we saw German blood pouring in the streets of Warsaw . . . we felt within us, great rejoicing.

was unclear, Hausner seemed to be drifting back into his role as an educator determined to show that Jews did resist. After this brief digression, the prosecution rested its case.

The Trial as a Testament

With the retelling of survivors' harrowing experiences, the Eichmann trial became more than just law and evidence, more than just determination of a man's guilt or innocence. It had become a reliving of the Holocaust. Hausner later wrote "It was often excruciating merely to listen to one of these tales. Sometimes we felt as if our reactions were paralyzed, and we were benumbed." [61]

The prosecutors sometimes heard loud sobs from the crowded courtroom. People occasionally fainted and had to be carried out. Newspaper reporters had to leave after an hour or two, unable to take more without a break. The strain of the trial was causing people to become jumpy and exhausted.

Eichmann listened closely to the testimony throughout his trial, but he rarely expressed any emotions.

Eichmann never seemed bothered by what he was hearing, though he paid close attention to the testimony. Hausner wrote, "Eichmann displayed no sign of being affected. . . . He followed the evidence intently. . . . His eyes would watch the witnesses, observe the judges for their impressions, and look as far as the defense and prosecution tables. He almost never looked into the courtroom." [62]

There was a certain irony to the prosecution case against Eichmann. The more dramatic the testimony, the less it seemed to relate to Eichmann. The highest drama came from descriptions of the work of the Einsatzgruppen in eastern Europe. But most of the Einsatzgruppen's victims lived near the place where they were killed. Eichmann specialized in moving victims to killing grounds. He seemed far removed from those who did the killing. Hausner hoped the judges and his worldwide audience would not see Eichmann as too far removed. The prosecution had tried to show that administrative efficiency was a murderous talent equally worthy of condemnation as the actual killing. Hausner and his team wondered if they had succeeded.

Chapter 5

The Case for the Defense

THE PROSECUTION'S CASE HAD LASTED fifty-six days. The judges then gave the defense a week to prepare its case. The defense case began on June 20, 1961, the seventy-fifth session of the trial.

The basic strategy of Eichmann's defense attorney, Robert Servatius, was to insist that Eichmann's actions during World War II were responses to direct orders. Although the "following orders" defense had been rejected as insufficient justification for criminal acts by the judges at the Nuremberg trials, Servatius chose it as the focus of Eichmann's defense.

Despite prosecutor Hausner's inability to directly connect a fair amount of the evidence to Eichmann, his case was strong. Servatius could not deny the Holocaust. He had not subjected prosecution witnesses to the tough and probing cross-examination one expects in a murder trial, since he was not denying what they said. He had rarely even asked witnesses to clarify details. Servatius had, on occasion, questioned the relevance of documents to the case. Eichmann's defense, rather than denying Eichmann's connection to the crimes, did deny Eichmann's responsibility for the crimes of which he was charged. Eichmann was a mere transmitter of orders, the defense claimed, with no power and no desire to act on his own. This was the essence of the defense case.

Servatius, like Hausner, followed customary trial practice and delivered an opening statement. The first paragraph of his statement showed the approach he would take:

In this case two worlds are opposing each other—the
world of the sufferers and the world of the rulers, the victims and the machinery of the dictator, those above and
those below. Tears are unknown in the world of the Cae-
sars. The Defence will describe the dictator's machinery
and the place held therein by the Accused. It will be
shown that the insertion of the Accused into the process
of persecution of the Jews was the necessary and, as far
as the Accused is concerned, inevitable result of the
political intention of the State's leadership. It will
become clear that the accusation of the Accused having
been worse than Hitler, is a construction made *ex post
facto* [after the fact]. It will emerge that the allegation of
the Accused having willfully sabotaged the orders of his
superiors calling for moderation, is . . . untrue.[63]

*Robert Servatius
conducted little cross-
examination of witnesses
during the prosecution's
case, as he did not deny the
events of the Holocaust.
Rather, his defense centered
on the argument that
Eichmann was merely
following direct orders
and had no power to act
independently.*

Next Servatius addressed the issue of whether his client would testify in his own defense. Eichmann had been informed by the judges that he could make a statement without being sworn in, or make a statement under oath. If he chose the latter, he would be subject to cross-examination. He could also, as is customary under the Anglo-Saxon system on which Israeli law is based, remain silent. In this system of laws, an accused cannot be forced to testify. If the accused chooses to testify, however, he or she becomes a defense witness whom the prosecution can try to discredit. Servatius stated that Eichmann would testify

> with the full knowledge of the consequences of cross-examination. He will testify, knowing that during his interrogation in the preliminary proceedings held by the police, he has given a candid description of the events which conforms to the truth. . . .

> A proper illumination of the documents by the Defence, will show that the responsibility for the events is to be attributed to the political leadership alone. It will appear that the highest authorities of the State had created the basis for the persecution and the extermination. . . . These authorities [provided] the legal basis for the measures of persecution, in the absence of which the Accused could not have taken a single step. . . . The Defence will show that the Accused precisely did not belong to the dominant political leading class of the commanders, but he was a recipient of orders on a lower rank. . . .

> The Defence will prove that the Accused does not bear any responsibility for the exterminations which were carried out. It will become clear that they had neither been ordered nor executed by the Accused himself. . . .

> The Accused will comment on the alternative open to him to refuse the execution of orders given to him. It will emerge that for him no such alternative existed.[64]

Servatius then began to question Adolf Eichmann; more precisely, to ask short questions that allowed Eichmann to give lengthy answers. Servatius would also sometimes read parts of documents and ask Eichmann to comment.

Eichmann Testifies

As a witness, Eichmann was determined to minimize his role in the Holocaust. Basically, he claimed to be a train dispatcher, a man who made trains run on time. According to his testimony, Eichmann was not in a position to make decisions independently. He did not want to make such decisions. "I particularly made it a point not to take any decisions, no matter how minor, on my initiative. . . . I made absolutely sure to get instructions from my chief,"[65] Eichmann commented at one point.

All decisions were made at a higher level, Eichmann claimed. Any initiative shown in his department was shown by subordinates, who were somehow able to act without his orders. Eichmann personally never had any special authority or position.

Eichmann attempted to minimize his role in the Holocaust by claiming that he never had any authority and was merely a dispatcher who ensured that the trains ran on time.

It was a different matter, he claimed, with his deputy Rolf Guenther. (Guenther vanished at the end of World War II and could not be questioned.) Guenther received special assignments from Heinrich Mueller, chief of the Gestapo and Eichmann's superior. Eichmann claimed this could explain the section's involvement in areas outside its assigned tasks, such as how his office became involved in such matters as the supply of poison gas to the death camps.

Eichmann placed blame for orders issued by his department on his deputy, Rolf Guenther (pictured).

Eichmann admitted that many instructions, directives, and orders were issued by his department, and that many of these bore his signature. However, he claimed, his department only drafted orders for superiors on their instructions. If he signed the documents, this was also on the instruction of his superiors. Other documents bore the marks of his department solely for filing purposes, as his office was the central depository for records of Jewish affairs. Some documents he was sent he claimed never to have received.

According to Eichmann, documents that described or implied his role in various events or actions—important in the prosecution's case—were inaccurate or were forgeries, despite whatever official status the document may have had. Sometimes, Eichmann protested, his name was incorrectly inserted into an otherwise accurate document. For example, Servatius asked Eichmann about one particular document, concerning gas equipment for the death camps, a matter already brought up in the prosecution case. At the end of the first page, the document stated, "I would draw your attention to the fact that . . . Eich-mann, the official in charge of Jewish questions in the [RSHA], is in agreement with this procedure."[66] Eichmann first responded that his name did not appear in a handwritten draft of the document. He then claimed:

> In the clean-typed text after that, the name Eichmann has been inserted wrongly. It also appears in the actual draft and appears again in the final version of the draft. I can only say that, apparently, the official in charge was not aware at the time with whom he would really have to deal.[67]

Eichmann's defense attorney, Dr. Servatius, never denied the events of the Holocaust. There was little cross-examination of pros-ecution witnesses. The defense strategy during the trial was to min-imize Eichmann's involvement. What Eichmann did do was the result of following orders that he had no choice but to obey. The defense stressed this idea. In his memoirs of the trial, chief prose-cutor Hausner expressed his views on the effect of this strategy:

> It soon became clear that he would stop at nothing; he would not hesitate to describe himself as a nobody; to believe him, his superiors were endowed with phenom-enal capacities, his subordinates were far more active than he was, and the RSHA was so disorganized that it could never have functioned.[68]

According to the prosecutor, Eichmann sometimes claimed that he had already admitted much, and would not have denied a particular matter if it was true. In Hausner's estimation, Eich-mann simply wanted to appear more forthright and honest. As Hausner surmised, "A partial, usually less damaging, confession was to serve as warranty for the truthfulness of his whole testi-mony; otherwise, he would ask, . . . why should he have con-fessed at all?"[69]

Eichmann Claims to Support Zionism

Eichmann did confess to "helping" Jews emigrate from Europe. Early in his career in Austria, Eichmann claimed, he became

Eichmann refers to a chart of the German chain of command during his testimony. He repeatedly denied personal responsibility for his actions and claimed that documents presented by the prosecution were either inaccurate or forgeries.

interested in the Zionist movement, which advocated the creation of a separate state for Jews in what was then called Palestine. This, Eichmann claimed, was the reason he promoted emigration from Austria. His efforts came to an end with Kristallnacht, the violence against Jews in Germany and Austria in November 1938. Eichmann, however, claimed he had nothing to do with that night's violence. His goal was the peaceable establishment of a Jewish homeland.

Later in the trial, during cross-examination, prosecutors questioned why Eichmann received rapid reports of events during Kristallnacht, in particular why he received reports of burning synagogues at 2:30 A.M.? Eichmann claimed he was keeping files and archives in synagogue outbuildings and had to rescue the documents. Once the terror inspired by Kristallnacht showed no signs of abating, Eichmann testified that forced emigration became a way of saving Jews from certain death. Yet he

A synagogue that was destroyed during Kristallnacht. Despite evidence to the contrary, Eichmann denied any complicity in the Kristallnacht mayhem.

admitted under cross-examination that the murder of European Jews had not yet been contemplated by Nazi officials while he was in Austria; this made prosecutors believe that protecting Jews from certain death was not an honest motivation. Eichmann even admitted that the violence of Kristallnacht was quite helpful to him in prompting Austrian Jews to leave.

Eichmann's Style of Testimony

The defense questioning of Eichmann, and the cross-examination, provided an opportunity for those present in the courtroom to observe Eichmann under pressure. All searched for hints into his real personality. One immediate observation was Eichmann's speaking style. He tended to speak in long and confusing sentences, intentionally or unintentionally having trouble getting to the point. For example, when Servatius asked at what point Eichmann's section became concerned with more than just transportation, Eichmann responded that in the course of the progressive centralization efforts conditioned by events during the War, all Jewish matters were incorporated in . . . my Section—that is, all obligations, to the extent that they were of importance for Department IV [of the Gestapo]. . . . I became the official dealing with these matters. Nevertheless, an autonomous treatment of this question by an administrator within a single office was impossible in this case, since the problem was not decided only with the competence of that office.[70]

Translators were sorely tested in conveying Eichmann's words accurately to the court. Eventually, the German-speaking judges dispensed with translation into Hebrew. They listened directly to Eichmann's German, and later questioned him in German. Historian Tom Segev later described Eichmann's direct testimony over fourteen court sessions: "As a witness, Eichmann did himself little good. He spoke like someone who had been caught up in some sort of bureaucratic misunderstanding that had to be cleared up."[71] Eichmann did at times show flashes of anger during the prosecution's cross-examination. However, he usually showed little or no emotion.

Cross-Examination

Hausner's turn to question Eichmann came after Servatius finished. Hausner's style struck at least one observer as presenting a rather dramatic visual image:

Hausner . . . laced his questions with hostile sarcasm. Sometimes he stretched out his arm, pointing at the defendant, his black robe forming a triangle from his wrist to his belt. He looked like a huge raven—dark, frightening, very theatrical.[72]

In his memoir of the trial, Hausner wrote that his goal in cross-examination was to destroy Eichmann's story and deflate Eichmann. To do this, Hausner had to discredit the details of the accused's testimony, and thus discredit his defense. Step by step, Hausner questioned each aspect of Eichmann's testimony.

Hausner's cross-examination of Eichmann was forceful and often dramatic. At times he would point directly at the defendant, questioning him in a hostile, sarcastic tone.

Eichmann's Authority

During cross-examination, Hausner continually questioned Eichmann's claim that he did not have the authority to make independent decisions concerning the fate of the Jews. Hausner later wrote, "I distributed my questions on particulars concerning his status all through the cross-examination. This was obviously a preferable technique to a frontal encounter, which he would try to dodge." [73] Answering these questions, Eichmann provided a variety of explanations as to why he drafted or signed documents, always insisting he responded to the orders of someone else. Anyone who stated, or implied, that Eichmann could use his own initiative was lying and trying to make Eichmann the scapegoat.

Hausner asked Eichmann if he was satisfied with the results of the Wannsee Conference, the January 1942 meeting at which plans for the final solution were laid. Eichmann had organized and taken the minutes at this meeting. Eichmann responded that he was satisfied for a different reason than RSHA chief Heydrich, who ran the conference. Heydrich was satisfied over the results, that the organized murder of the Jews would run more smoothly. Eichmann felt secure in the knowledge that he had done all he could to promote emigration and was thus blameless if his superiors at the conference opted for more drastic measures. Eichmann said,

> [I] was reassured by the thought that, although I held a relatively low rank . . . I had striven to be on the look-out for possible solutions—possible peaceful solutions — which would be acceptable to both parties, but would not require such a violent and drastic solution of bloodshed. . . . I felt something of the satisfaction of Pilate, because I felt entirely innocent of any guilt. . . . The "Popes" had given their orders; it was up to me to obey.[74]

When ordered by his superiors, Eichmann had no choice but to abandon the peaceful solution of Jewish emigration and adhere to the new policy of organized mass murder.

REINHARD HEYDRICH

The tall, blue-eyed, blond Heydrich was one of the few higher-ranking Nazis who actually resembled the Nazi "Aryan" ideal. Reinhard Heydrich, born in Prussia in 1904, was the son of a singer and director of a conservatory. Heydrich had originally joined the German navy, but was thrown out for conduct unbecoming an officer (breach of promise). In 1932, soon after he joined the SS, Heydrich was assigned by SS chief Heinrich Himmler to form a security service, the SD. Heydrich worked as Himmler's right-hand man to centralize control of all German policy functions. In 1939 Heydrich became head of the newly formed RSHA, the Reich Central Security Office, in charge of all SS functions (including the secret state police, the Gestapo) with the exception of Waffen-SS combat troops. Heydrich managed Nazi terror, including the murder of the Jews. Eichmann was Heydrich's best-known subordinate.

In September 1941, Heydrich assumed the additional title of Deputy Reich Protector of Bohemia and Moravia, the parts of Czechoslovakia not directly annexed by Germany. In May 1942, Heydrich was severely wounded in an assassination attempt by Czech partisans. He died eight days later.

The cross-examination had lasted two weeks. Hausner later wrote that he hoped it "had achieved the objective of destroying the image of a 'victim of orders,' who never overstepped his duties." [75] Eichmann had not been able to overcome the image presented by the prosecution that though he did receive orders he enthusiastically exceeded these orders in pursuit of the ultimate goal of killing the Jews.

Redirect Examination and Judges' Questioning

Servatius conducted a brief re-cross-examination of Eichmann after cross-examination was completed, adding little to what was brought out earlier.

Then the judges had a turn to question Eichmann. Under Israeli procedure and custom, following the British example, judges are permitted to question defendants. Unlike the prosecution, or the defense, judges have an obligation to be objective. (American judges, though permitted to question witnesses, rarely do so.)

Judge Raveh (right) questions Eichmann (left) in an attempt to clarify inconsistencies in his testimony.

HANNAH ARENDT ON THE JUDGES

Hannah Arendt's reports on the Eichmann trial, collected as *Eichmann in Jerusalem*, challenged the prosecution but complimented the judges for their conduct and objectivity.

At no time is there anything theatrical in the conduct of the judges. Their walk is unstudied, their sober and intense attention, visibly stiffening under the impact of grief as they listen to the tales of suffering, is natural; their impatience with the prosecutor's attempt to drag out these hearings forever is spontaneous and refreshing, their attitude to the defense perhaps a shade over-polite . . . their manner toward the accused always beyond reproach.

The judges questioned Eichmann in an attempt to clarify inconsistencies in his testimony. How, for example, could senior officers not even make suggestions to their superiors? Eichmann said that he never made suggestions. In a response to a judge's question about the inherent connection between Nazi doctrine and anti-Semitism, Eichmann claimed that anti-Semitism was not an integral part of Nazism. In response to another question on statements made at the Wannsee Conference, Eichmann said he was too busy taking notes to hear what was being said.

Eichmann's responses, judging from the sometimes tough follow-up questions the judges asked, did not satisfy the panel. The judges' reactions to Eichmann's testimony would be clear in their verdict. But it was not only the judges who were stunned by what they heard. Hausner later wrote, "an atmosphere of utter disbelief came to reign throughout the courtroom." [76]

Witnesses from Abroad

Defense witnesses "testified" after the rest of the defense case, cross-examination, and judges' questioning was over. The witnesses did not actually appear in court, but sworn statements were presented immediately following the judges' questioning and continued to be entered into evidence over the next few sessions of the trial.

For various reasons, the witnesses either could not or would not come to Israel. Most were former Nazis and were either subject to arrest under the same laws used to try Eichmann, or feared they were subject. Hausner could not grant safe conduct to these witnesses (with two exceptions, who refused to come to Israel anyway) nor could he force witnesses to come to Israel, though there was no particular reason for a prosecutor to want to compel defense witnesses to testify. The judges made it clear they would prefer to have witnesses testify in person but they accepted the absentee statements.

Eichmann's witnesses would appear in court where they lived, and give depositions (sworn legal statements) in the presence of defense and prosecution representatives. Hausner worried that the witnesses, presumed to be favorable to Eichmann, would have the chance to lie without the prosecution being able to cross-examine. Even if they did not lie, they could stretch and alter the truth to be most favorable to Eichmann.

When the statements were read in court, Hausner was pleasantly surprised. He later wrote that,

> . . . . none of the witnesses went along all the way with Eichmann's version [of his role in the Holocaust]. To be sure, some of them made a marked attempt to be helpful to him and were obviously inclined to picture his activities in a more favorable light, but even they supported him only up to a point and would not go very far.[77]

One witness was Edmund Veesenmeyer, an official of the German Foreign Ministry assigned to the Hungarian capital of Budapest. His statement included such lines as "I knew that the Eichmann Special Commando was engaged in the deportations of Jews. . . . As to Eichmann's powers, I myself had no knowledge."[78] Veesenmeyer also claimed not to have known why Eichmann was in Budapest, and not to have received any instructions on his own assignment. His statement was so full of inconsistencies that when Servatius called him a liar, Hausner did not argue.

Another defense witness was Eberhard von Thadden, chief of the Jewish Affairs Department at the German Foreign Ministry and Eichmann's contact at that ministry. In a report he wrote during the war, von Thadden indicated that

Eberhard von Thadden, chief of the Jewish Affairs Department at the German Foreign Ministry, was one of a number of defense witnesses whose testimony was taken by deposition in their home countries.

the Eichmann Special Operations Unit in Hungary was acting in accordance with a definite plan. I could not determine to what extent Eichmann had co-ordinated this plan with other authorities. I myself was horrified at the plan which Eichmann disclosed to me. . . . As far as I know, the plan was not implemented in the form disclosed to me originally by Eichmann when I saw him in Budapest. According to the original plan, the Jewish population of Budapest was to be herded together one night on an island in the Danube and interned there, without adequate preparation.[79]

On the next page of his affidavit, von Thadden stated, apparently referring either to a change in plans or the next step after the island internment, "Regarding the evacuation of the Jews from Hungary, it was always said that they were to be deported to the Eastern Occupied Territories. The name of the Auschwitz Camp was also mentioned in this context." [80] The testimony of these absentee witnesses failed to bolster Eichmann's defense. Servatius's tactic ended up buoying the confidence of the prosecution.

With the presentation of evidence from abroad, the main part of the trial was over. On August 8, 1961, the prosecution and defense would deliver their closing summations.

Chapter 6

Summations, Sentencing, Results

AFTER THE DEFENSE RESTED its case and the prosecution had cross-examined Eichmann, the two sides gave final summations. Both defense and prosecution reviewed their cases before the judges, stressing the high points, declaring that they proved what they had set out to prove.

Prosecution Summation

Gideon Hausner began his final statement with the following:

> If it please the court, in this trial there has unfolded before our eyes the image of a regime which, in our generation, threatened to put an end to the liberty of man and to the liberty of nations. In particular, there hovered here, within the walls of this court-room, the shades of Adolf Hitler and his band of accomplices, those semblances of horror which mankind will recall forever as the embodiment of wickedness to the depths of the abyss.[81]

Hausner reviewed his case, summarizing the extensive evidence he had presented against Eichmann. He spoke of the Holocaust, in which Eichmann played so central a part: "I believe that if anyone were to try to invent a nightmare, he would be incapable of describing even a small fraction of the shocking and terrible occurrences that were related, described and presented here."[82]

Hausner reviewed Eichmann's connection to the atrocities. Eichmann did not create the anti-Jewish measures of the Third Reich, the escalating series of crimes leading up to the final solution. Eichmann was not the only person to play a role in these crimes. However, Eichmann was one of the key individuals. He greased the wheels to make everything run better. He had been given orders and not only enthusiastically followed these orders but added to them, finding better ways of carrying them out.

Hausner discussed the "following orders" defense employed by defense attorney Servatius. He noted that obeying manifestly illegal orders is not a valid defense, and again noted that this excuse had already been rejected during the Nuremberg trials.

Defense Summation

Servatius spoke after Hausner. Following German procedure, Servatius had already submitted a lengthy brief summarizing the defense case. The defense argument in the final statement was that Eichmann's role was exaggerated. Servatius insisted that the

The hands of Adolf Eichmann, the hands that "greased the wheels" of the Nazi machinery of mass murder. During closing arguments, Hausner emphasized that Eichmann did not merely follow orders, but did so eagerly and efficiently.

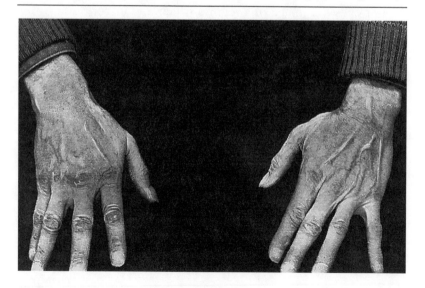

prosecution case made it appear that Eichmann was solely responsible for the Holocaust. But Eichmann was not responsible. He had received orders from his superiors, and as a soldier he could not refuse to follow these orders. Servatius argued that his client had done nothing to expedite any matter relating the Holocaust. He did only what he was ordered to do.

After Servatius tendered his brief, the judges adjourned on August 14, 1961, to reach their verdict. The trial had lasted 114 sessions.

The Verdict

The judges handed down their verdict at the next session of the court, which was slated for the morning of December 11, 1961, roughly four months after the end of summations.

The judges called the court to order and announced that they found Eichmann guilty on all charges and counts, except for the charges that Eichmann aided the murder of ninety-three children from Lidice, Czechoslovakia. The judges found no justification for Eichmann's actions, and specifically rejected the "following orders" defense. They found no extenuating circumstances that would lessen his guilt. Four days later, after statements from Hausner requesting the death penalty and a final statement by the accused, still professing his innocence, Adolf Eichmann was sentenced to death.

Appeal and Aftermath

Israeli law requires automatic appeals of death sentences to the Israeli Supreme Court. Eichmann's case was the first instance in which this law was used. (The only other time was in 1993, when the conviction of John Demjanjuk on Nazi war crimes was overturned.) Briefs were filed with the Supreme Court and arguments presented before that Court on March 22, 1962. Judgment was delivered on May 29, 1962, upholding the verdict and sentence. Eichmann immediately appealed to the president of Israel for mercy, offering the same arguments from the earlier rounds of the judicial procedures. The minister of justice also filed an opinion with the president, supporting the verdict and the sentence.

⚖️ EICHMANN'S FINAL STATEMENT TO THE COURT

After being convicted, and after Hausner and Servatius addressed the question of penalty, Adolf Eichmann made a final statement to the court at the end of the 120th session of the trial (Wednesday, December 13, 1961). Taken from the court transcripts, selections from Eichmann's statement follow:

I have heard the Court's severe verdict of guilty. I see myself disappointed in my hopes for justice. I cannot recognize the verdict of guilty. I understand the demand for atonement for the crimes which were perpetrated against the Jews. The witnesses' statements here in the Court made my limbs go numb once again, just as they went numb when once, acting on orders, I had to look at the atrocities. It was my misfortune to become entangled in these atrocities. But these misdeeds did not happen according to my wishes. It was not my wish to slay people. The guilt for the mass murder is solely that of the political leaders. . . .

My life's principle, which I was taught very early on, was to desire and to strive to achieve ethical values. From a particular moment on, however, I was prevented by the State from living according to that principle. . . .

I am not the monster I am made out to be. I am the victim of an error of judgement. [Eichmann's kidnapping and trial] can quite obviously only be explained by the fact that I was considered to be the person who was responsible for everything. The reason for this lies in the fact that the National Socialists of the time and others have spread untruths about me. They wanted to exonerate themselves at my expense, or to create confusion for reasons unknown to me. . . . This is the cause of the false inference. This is the reason I am here.

Controversy over the Death Sentence

The Israeli judicial system had never imposed the death sentence before, nor has it done so since. Even for a man such as Adolf Eichmann, the first state imposition of the death penalty created controversy.

In May 1962 Shmuel Hugo Bergmann, a seventy-eight-year-old professor of philosophy at Hebrew University in Jerusalem, sent a petition to Israeli president Yitzhak Ben-Zvi asking for clemency in Eichmann's case. The signers, including Martin Buber, a well-known philosopher living in Israel, made this plea:

We are not pleading for his life, because we know that no man is less worthy than he of mercy, and we are not asking you to pardon him. We ask for your decision [to commute the execution] for the sake of our country and the sake of our people. Our belief is that concluding Eichmann's trial with his execution will diminish the image of the Holocaust and falsify the historical and moral significance of this trial.

We do not want the nemesis [enemy] to bring us to the point where we appoint a hangman from among us; if we do so it will be a victory for the nemesis, and we do not wish such a victory. The haters of Israel around the world want us to be caught in this trap. Carrying out a death sentence will make it possible for them to claim that the crime of the Nazis has been paid for, that blood ransom has been paid to the Jewish people for the blood that was shed. Let us not lend our hands to this; let us not agree, or even imply that we agree, that it is possible to ransom the sacrifice of six million by the hanging of this evil man.[83]

There is no indication of a direct response to the petition from the president. Ben-Zvi also rejected Eichmann's appeal. Eichmann was hanged just before midnight on May 31, 1962. In his last words he thanked Germany, Argentina, and

Eichmann in captivity in April 1961, before being tried for his war crimes.

Austria (for what he did not say) and added that during wartime he had felt compelled to obey the rule of law and his flag. The Israelis ordered his body to be cremated and his ashes scattered in the Mediterranean, well beyond Israeli territorial waters.

Reaction to the Trial

The trial exposed the horrors of the Holocaust to the world. Hausner's education strategy worked. His was not a perfect case, sometimes leaning too far toward spectacle and away from establishing guilt, but most observers felt Hausner had connected Eichmann to the Holocaust sufficiently to warrant the guilty verdict and the death sentence.

The Eichmann trial brought the Holocaust to the forefront in Israel. Hausner began receiving letters even before the trial

Yad Vashem, the memorial in Jerusalem to the six million Jews who perished at the hands of the Nazis.

THE BERGMANN LETTER

Professor Shmuel Hugo Bergmann, professor of philosophy at Hebrew University, wrote to three former students regarding his effort to organize a petition for clemency for Eichmann. The following excerpt appears in Tom Segev's *The Seventh Million.*

I oppose the death penalty in any form. That people learned in the law would sit together tranquilly and decide, with cold and objective consideration, that a man should be hanged—and that not they, but some other man paid a fee for it, would hang him—that is in my eyes the utmost cruelty. Who gave them permission to take life, and in so doing to take from the defendant the possibility of doing penance for his sins while he is still in this world? Only he who creates life has the authority to take life. . . .

As for the man himself, the death penalty is a much more lenient punishment than lifetime imprisonment in an Israeli jail. Given the horrible crime he committed, there is no fit punishment for him. . . .

I believe with perfect faith the clemency for this man will halt the chain of hatred and bring the world a bit of salvation.

ended: "A girl [living in Israel] wrote saying she had no uncles and aunts to visit on Saturdays and holidays, like the other children, but had never understood before why they were all dead." [84]

This portion of the past was brought to light as it had not been in the early years of the state. As Israeli historian Tom Segev later wrote in his study of Israel and the Holocaust:

Never had Israel lived the horror of the Holocaust as it did in these months. . . . The Eichmann trial marked the beginning of a dramatic shift in the way Israelis related to the Holocaust. The terrifying stories that broke forth from the depths of silence brought about a process of identification with the suffering of the victims and the survivors. [85]

Finally, the Eichmann trial was about the ultimate defeat of ultimate evil. It was about the triumph of the chief victims of Nazi Germany, the Jews, over their persecutors. In his memoir of the trial, written several years later, Gideon Hausner summarized its significance:

THE TRIAL WAS ESSENTIAL

Gideon Hausner included press coverage in an appendix to his book on the trial, *Justice in Jerusalem*. He praised an article from the February 1962 *Atlantic Monthly* as an excellent summary of the trial.

> The trial was essential, to every human being now alive, and to all who follow us; and, despite its length, its carefulness, the trial furnishes only a partial record—for the scene of the crime was a whole continent, the victims were a whole nation, the methodical savages who committed the crimes were as clever as they were evil, ingenious, brilliant organizers, addicts to paperwork. This is the best record we and our descendants will ever have; and we owe the state of Israel an immeasurable debt for proving it. No one who tries to understand our times, now or in the future, can overlook this documentation of a way of life and death which will stain our century forever. No one will see the complete dimensions of twentieth-century man— and that includes all of us, I insist—without studying the Eichmann trial.

Now it was the Jews themselves who could decide what was best for their position. They could do so because they had their own machinery of justice, their own prosecutors and their own policemen. The trial was thus, in itself, an overwhelming manifestation of the revolution in the position of the Jewish people that has taken place in this generation.[86]

The trial of Adolf Eichmann may not have dispelled the ghosts of Hitler and his accomplices. The more recent genocidal campaigns in Bosnia ("ethnic cleansing" of thousands of Bosnian Muslims by Bosnian Serbs) and Cambodia (the murder of 2 million out of 8 million Cambodians by their own government) make this terribly clear. However, the trial at least made the world more aware of these ghosts. Whether Eichmann was a monster, an obsessed bureaucrat, or both, the trial provided a vivid record of how men who put their conscience aside can do as much damage as perpetrators of evil deeds.

Notes

Introduction

1. Hannah Arendt, *Eichmann in Jerusalem: A Report on the Banality of Evil*: Revised and enlarged edition, New York: Penguin Books, 1977, page 209. (Revised edition first published Viking books 1965.)
2. Knesset Proceedings, XXIX: 2106, 8 August 1960, quoted in Tom Segev, *The Seventh Million: The Israelis and the Holocaust*. New York: Hill and Wang, 1993, p. 333.
3. Gabriel Strassman, "What Did the Eichmann Trial Give Us?" *Maariv*, December 11, 1981, quoted in Segev, *The Seventh Million*, p. 351.
4. Isser Harel, *The House on Garibaldi Street*. New York: Viking, 1975, p. 85.

Chapter 1: The Capture of Adolf Eichmann

5. Quoted in William L. Shirer, *The Rise and Fall of the Third Reich*. New York: Simon and Schuster, 1960, p. 978.
6. Harel, *The House on Garibaldi Street*, rev., ed., and with an introduction by Shlomo J. Shpiro. London: Frank Cass, 1997, p. 8.
7. Quoted in Harel, *The House on Garibaldi Street*, 1975, p. 19.
8. Quoted in Harel, *The House on Garibaldi Street*, 1975, pp. 19–20
9. Quoted in Harel, *The House on Garibaldi Street*, 1975, p. 20
10. Quoted in Harel, *The House on Garibaldi Street*, 1975, p. 35.
11. Peter Z. Malkin and Harry Stein, *Eichmann in My Hands*, New York: Warner Books, 1990, p. 108.
12. Harel, *The House on Garibaldi Street*, 1975, p. 167.
13. Quoted in Malkin and Stein, *Eichmann in My Hands*, p. 190.
14. Quoted in Segev, *The Seventh Million*, p. 326.
15. Quoted in Harel, *The House on Garibaldi Street*, 1997, p. 284.

Chapter 2: Preparing the Case

16. United Nations War Crimes Commission, *Law Reports of Trials of War Criminals*, vol. 15, *Digest of Laws and Cases*. London: United Nations, 1949, p. 26.

17. Ben-Gurion to Frondizi, June 3, 1960, reprinted in "Eichmann in the World Press," Israel Ministry for Foreign Affairs, Information Division, Jerusalem, July 1960, pp. i–ii.
18. *El Mundo* (Buenos Aires), June 17, 1960, quoted in "Eichmann in the World Press," pp. 1.
19. *Boston Record American*, June 23, 1960, quoted in American Jewish Committee, "The Eichmann Case in the American Press." New York: Institute of Human Relations Press, n.d., p. 10.
20. *Frankfurter Allgemeine Zeitung*, May 25, 1960, quoted in "Eichmann in the World Press," p. 69.
21. Gideon Hausner, *Justice in Jerusalem*. New York: Harper and Row, 1966, p. 289.
22. *Frankfurter Allgemeine Zeitung*, February 28, 1961, quoted in American Jewish Committee, "The Eichmann Case: Moral Questions and Legal Arguments." New York: American Jewish Committee, 1961, p. 7.
23. Ben-Gurion to Yitzhak Y. Cohen, April 10, 1961, quoted in Segev, *The Seventh Million*, p. 327.
24. Quoted in Segev, *The Seventh Million*, p. 98.
25. Hausner, *Justice in Jerusalem*, p. 291.
26. Hausner, *Justice in Jerusalem*, p. 291.
27. Malkin and Stein, *Eichmann in My Hands*, p. 216.
28. Hausner, *Justice in Jerusalem*, p. 278.
29. Jochen von Lang and Claus Sibyll, eds., *Eichmann Interrogated: Transcripts from the Archives of the Israeli Police*, trans. Ralph Manheim, introduction by Avner W. Less. New York: Farrar, Straus & Giroux, 1983, p. 38.
30 Von Lang and Sibyll, *Eichmann Interrogated*, p. 144.
31. Von Lang and Sibyll, *Eichmann Interrogated*, p. 145.
32. Von Lang and Sibyll, *Eichmann Interrogated*, p. 252–53,
33. Von Lang and Sibyll, *Eichmann Interrogated*, p. 138.
34. Hausner, *Justice in Jerusalem*, p. 298.
35. Hausner, *Justice in Jerusalem*, p. 298.

Chapter 3: The Trial Opens

36. Hausner, *Justice in Jerusalem*, p. 309.
37. Hausner, *Justice in Jerusalem*, p. 309.

38. State of Israel, Ministry of Justice, *The Trial of Adolf Eichmann: Record of Proceedings in the District Court of Jerusalem,* Jerusalem, 1992–1994, vol. 1, p. 8. (Henceforth, "Eichmann Trial Proceedings.")

39. Eichmann Trial Proceedings, vol. 1, p. 8.

40. Michael Patrick Murray, *A Study in Public International Law: Comparing the Trial of Adolf Eichmann in Jerusalem with the Trial of the Major German War Criminals at Nuremberg,* unpublished dissertation, Washington, DC: National Law Center of the George Washington University, June 1973, pp. V–10, V–11.

41. Quoted in Hausner, *Justice in Jerusalem,* p. 312.

42. Hausner, *Justice in Jerusalem,* p. 312.

43. Quoted in Hausner, *Justice in Jerusalem,* p. 313.

44. Quoted in Hausner, *Justice in Jerusalem,* pp. 316–17.

45. Hausner, *Justice in Jerusalem,* p. 318.

46. Eichmann Trial Proceedings, vol. 1, p. 60.

47. Quoted in Hausner, *Justice in Jerusalem,* p. 295.

48. Eichmann Trial Proceedings, vol. 1, p. 62.

49. Eichmann Trial Proceedings, vol. 1, p. 62.

50. Hausner, *Justice in Jerusalem,* p. 325.

51. Quoted in Hausner, *Justice in Jerusalem,* p. 325.

Chapter 4: The Prosecution Presents Its Case

52. Eichmann Trial Proceedings, vol. 1, p. 398

53. Eichmann Trial Proceedings, vol. 1, pp. 397–98.

54. Hannah Arendt, *Eichmann in Jerusalem: A Report on the Banality of Evil.* New York: Penguin Books, 1994, pp. 121–22.

55. Eichmann Trial Proceedings, vol. 1, pp. 516–17.

56. Eichmann Trial Proceedings, vol. 1, pp. 517–18.

57. Eichmann Trial Proceedings, vol. 1, p. 518.

58. Hausner, *Justice in Jerusalem,* p. 74.

59. Quoted in Steven Paskuly, ed. *Rudolph Hoess, Death Dealer: The Memoirs of the SS Kommandant at Auschwitz,* trans. Andrew Pollinger. Buffalo: Prometheus Books, 1992, p. 163.

60. Eichmann Trial Proceedings, vol. 3, p. 1005.

61. Hausner, *Justice in Jerusalem,* p. 331.

62. Hausner, *Justice in Jerusalem*, p. 332.

Chapter 5: The Case for the Defense

63. Eichmann Trial Proceedings, vol. 4, p. 1371
64. Eichmann Trial Proceedings, vol. 4, pp. 1371–1372.
65. Eichmann Trial Proceedings, vol. 4, p. 1424.
66. Eichmann Trial Proceedings, vol. 4, p. 1418.
67. Eichmann Trial Proceedings, vol. 4, p. 1418.
68. Hausner, *Justice in Jerusalem*, p. 353.
69. Hausner, *Justice in Jerusalem*, p. 355.
70. Eichmann Trial Proceedings, vol. 4, pp. 1378–79.
71. Segev, *The Seventh Million*, p. 354.
72. Segev, *The Seventh Million*, p. 355.
73. Hausner, *Justice in Jerusalem*, p. 360.
74. Eichmann Trial Proceedings, vol. 4, p. 1423.
75. Hausner, *Justice in Jerusalem*, p. 368.
76. Hausner, *Justice in Jerusalem*, p. 373.
77. Hausner, *Justice in Jerusalem*, pp. 375–76.
78. Eichmann Trial Proceedings, vol. 5, p. 1843.
79. Eichmann Trial Proceedings, vol. 4, p. 1525.
80. Eichmann Trial Proceedings, vol. 4, p. 1525.

Chapter 6: Summations, Sentencing, Results

81. Eichmann Trial Proceedings, vol. 5, p. 1973.
82. Eichmann Trial Proceedings, vol. 5, p. 1973.
83. Quoted in Segev, *The Seventh Million*, pp. 363–64.
84. Hausner, *Justice in Jerusalem*, p. 433.
85. Segev, *The Seventh Million*, p. 361.
86. Hausner, *Justice in Jerusalem*, p. 453.

For Further Reading

Eleanor H. Ayer, *Inferno: July 1943–April 1945*. Woodbridge, CT: Blackbirch Press, 1988. This book describes the experience of Jewish children during the most intense period of the Holocaust.

John Bradley, *The Illustrated History of the Third Reich*. New York: Grosset and Dunlap, 1987. A comprehensive, illustrated history of Nazi Germany that attaches faces to many of the people and places of the Holocaust.

Saul Friedlander, *Nazi Germany and the Jews*. Vol. 1. New York: HarperCollins, 1997. The first volume of a lengthy study of Nazi Germany and the Jews, this work makes use of newly available archives. The author looks both at policy making and the effects of this policy on individuals.

G. M. Gilbert, *Nuremberg Diary*. New York: Farrar, Straus & Giroux, 1961. An account of the 1946 Nuremberg trials of the senior Nazi leadership and examination of the defendants' motivations. Gilbert was a witness at the Eichmann trial.

Martin Gilbert, *The Holocaust*. New York: Holt, Rinehart and Winston, 1985. A complete history of the Holocaust by a major British military historian.

Israel Gutman, *Resistance: The Warsaw Ghetto Uprising*. Boston: Houghton Mifflin, 1994. A well-documented history of the major example of Jewish resistance to the Nazis.

Raul Hilberg, *Perpetrators, Victims, Bystanders*. New York: Aaron Asher Books, HarperCollins, 1992. An interesting collection of essays examining different groups of people involved in the Holocaust.

Dan Raviv and Yossi Melman, *Every Spy a Prince: The Complete Story of Israel's Intelligence Community*. Boston: Houghton Mifflin, 1990. This is a first-rate history of the Israeli intelligence community, including Mossad, the Shin Bet (in charge of domestic security, considered the rough equivalent of the FBI), and Aman (military intelligence), up to 1990. The

book provides additional context to the capture of Adolf
Eichmann.

Earle Rice Jr., *The Nuremberg Trials*. San Diego: Lucent Books,
1997. A quick but informative overview of the 1945–1946 trials of the high-level Nazi German leadership.

Gita Sereny, *Albert Speer: His Battle with Truth*. New York: Knopf,
1995. A lengthy study of a man trying to regain his lost conscience. Hitler's architect, Albert Speer, was one of the few
senior Nazis to admit guilt after World War II. This documents his struggle to understand his role in Nazi Germany.

Works Consulted

Avi Aharoni and Wilhelm Dietl, *Operation Eichmann*. Trans. Helmut Bögler. New York: John Wiley & Sons, 1997. A recent memoir of the Eichmann case by the Israeli agent who conclusively located Eichmann in Argentina. Aharoni also served on the team that actually captured Eichmann.

American Jewish Committee, "The Eichmann Case in the American Press." New York: Institute of Human Relations Press, n.d. Valuable summary of American press coverage of the Eichmann trial.

American Jewish Committee, "The Eichmann Case: Moral and Legal Arguments," n.d. A good, brief summary of trial issues with appropriate quotations, for those unable to research the lengthy commentary.

Hannah Arendt, *Eichmann in Jerusalem: A Report on the Banality of Evil*. New York: Penguin Books, 1994. First published as a series of articles for the *New Yorker* in 1963, philosopher Arendt's observations of the Eichmann trial provoked considerable controversy. Arendt considers Eichmann to have been guilty, but criticizes the prosecution's presentation of its case.

Roselle K. Chartock and Jack Spencer, eds. *Can It Happen Again? Chronicles of the Holocaust*. New York: Black Dog and Leventhal, 1995. Scholarly analysis of the Holocaust and its aftermath.

Lucy S. Dawidowicz, *The War Against the Jews*. New York: Holt, Rinehart and Winston, 1975. An exhaustive documentary study. Still a classic in its field.

Jacques Derogy and Hesi Carmel, *The Untold History of Israel*. New York: Grove Press, 1979. The history of the Israeli intelligence service.

"Eichmann in the World Press," Israel Ministry for Foreign Affairs, Information Division, Jerusalem, July 1960. World press reaction to Eichmann's capture.

117

Azriel Eisenberg, ed. *Witness to the Holocaust*. New York: Pilgrim Press, 1981. Interesting source of firsthand observations on the Holocaust and its aftermath.

Klaus P. Fischer, *Nazi Germany: A New History*. New York: Continuum, 1995. Accurately described as a comprehensive, richly narrated history of Nazi Germany.

Martha Gellhorn, "Eichmann and the Private Conscience," *Atlantic Monthly*, vol. 209, no. 2, February 1962. One of the journalists covering the Eichmann trial reports, for an American magazine, the facts and lessons of the trial.

Israel Gutman, ed., *Encyclopedia of the Holocaust*. New York: Macmillan, 1990. Valuable source of brief descriptions of people, organizations, and concepts of the Holocaust and the years leading up to the Holocaust.

Isser Harel, *The House on Garibaldi Street*. New York: Viking, 1975. The story of the capture of Eichmann from the man who led the effort. Harel was chief of Mossad, the legendary Israeli secret service, when Eichmann was located and captured.

Isser Harel, *The House on Garibaldi Street*. Rev. ed. Edited and with an introduction by Shlomo J. Shpiro. London: Frank Cass, 1997. Valuable updating, with new information, of Harel's 1975 work.

Gideon Hausner, *Justice in Jerusalem*. New York: Harper and Row, 1966. Best narrative of the trial with insights into the man who headed the prosecution.

Raul Hilberg, *The Destruction of the European Jews*. Rev. ed. New York: Holmes and Meier, 1985. This is a highly detailed three volume history of the Holocaust.

Jochen von Lang and Claus Sibyll, eds., *Eichmann Interrogated: Transcripts from the Archives of the Israeli Police*. Trans. Ralph Manheim. Introduction by Avner W. Less. New York: Farrar, Straus & Giroux, 1983. A valuable source in itself, as well as evidence introduced at Eichmann's trial.

Peter Z. Malkin and Harry Stein, *Eichmann in My Hands*. New York: Warner Books, 1990. The memoir of one of the Mossad agents who captured Eichmann. A valuable supporting narrative to Harel's description, Malkin provides insights into Eichmann's character.

Sybil Milton, trans., *The Stroop Report: The Jewish Quarter of Warsaw Is No More!* Introduction by Andrzej Wirth. New York: Pantheon Books, 1979. "Exemplary soldiers" killing innocent people who had the nerve to fight back.

Michael Patrick Murray, *A Study in Public International Law: Comparing the Trial of Adolf Eichmann in Jerusalem with the Trial of the Major German War Criminals at Nuremberg.* Unpublished dissertation. Washington, DC: National Law Center of the George Washington University, June 1973. A scholarly analysis of the legal issues of the trial.

Steven Paskuly, ed., *Rudolph Hoess, Death Dealer: The Memoirs of the SS Kommandant at Auschwitz.* Trans. Andrew Pollinger. Buffalo: Prometheus Books, 1992. Insight into a diabolical mind. Hoess killed the people Eichmann deported.

Shabtai Rosenne, ed., *6,000,000 Accusers: Israel's Case Against Eichmann, the Opening Speech and Legal Argument of Mr. Gideon Hausner, Attorney-General.* Jerusalem: Jerusalem Post, 1961. Initial publication of Hausner's opening arguments, this is useful backup to the official transcripts of the trial

Tom Segev, *1949: The First Israelis.* English language ed. Arlen Neal Weinstein. New York: The Free Press, 1986. A noted Israeli historian and journalist writes about life in the state of Israel in the years immediately after its independence in 1948.

Tom Segev, *The Seventh Million: The Israelis and the Holocaust.* New York: Hill and Wang, 1993. A valuable and definitive study of Israel and its reaction to the Holocaust. Translated by Haim Watzman, it provides access to work not otherwise available in English and examines the "image" of the Holocaust in Israel from the 1930s up to the 1991 Gulf War.

William L. Shirer, *The Rise and Fall of the Third Reich.* New York: Simon and Schuster, 1960. A masterpiece study of the Third

Reich up to the end of the 1946 Nuremberg trials. Eich-mann's capture is mentioned in an "as we went to press" footnote.

Albert Speer, *Inside the Third Reich*. Trans. Richard and Clara Winston. New York: Macmillan, 1970. The memoirs of Hitler's personal architect and city planner.

State of Israel, Ministry of Justice, *The Trial of Adolf Eichmann: Record of Proceedings in the District Court of Jerusalem*. 8 vols. Jerusalem, 1992–1994. The unadulterated record of the trial; an essential source for any student of the subject.

United Nations War Crimes Commission, *Law Reports of Trials of War Criminals*, Vol. 15, *Digest of Laws and Cases*. London: United Nations, 1949. Summaries of cases, laws, and prece-dents involved in the Nuremberg series of war crime trials.

Simon Wiesenthal, *The Murderers Among Us*. Edited, with a pro-file of the author, by Joseph Wechesberg. London: Heine-mann, 1967. Wiesenthal is a survivor of the Holocaust. This book details his work as the chief Nazi hunter outside of government, gathering facts on surviving senior Nazis.

Simon Wiesenthal, *The Sunflower*. Rev. ed. New York: Schocken Books, 1997. The subtitle tells it all: "On the possibilities and limits of forgiveness." Includes commentary by several philosophers, writers, and other public figures.

Christian Zentner and Friedemann Befurftig, eds. *The Encyclope-dia of the Third Reich*. English translation edited by Amy Hacket. New York: Macmillan, 1991. An excellent general reference encyclopedia.

Index

Picture Credits

Cover photo: AP/Wide World Photos

Archive Photos, 9, 17, 24, 73 (left), 86, 90, 93, 96, 98

Archives of the Simon Wiesenthal Center, 11, 75

Corbis, 54

Deutschland Erwacht/Simon Wiesenthal Center Archives of Los Angeles, 73 (right)

Express Newspapers/Archive Photos, 51

Express Newspapers/G496/Archive Photos, 45, 52 (center, right), 56

Express Newspapers/G607/Archive Photos, 27

International News Photos, 64

London Daily Express/Archive Photos, 13, 69

Main Commission for the Investigation of Nazi War Crimes, courtesy of United States Holocaust Memorial Museum Photo Archives, 77, 78, 83 (right)

National Archives, 83 (left), 84

National Archives, courtesy of United States Holocaust Memorial Museum Photo Archives, 72

Pictorial Parade, Inc./Archive Photos, 52 (left)

State Museum of Auschwitz-Birkenau, courtesy of United States Holocaust Memorial Museum Photo Archives, 81

UPI/Corbis-Bettmann, 12, 21, 23, 33, 35, 36, 38, 42, 49, 50, 63 (both), 66, 70, 71, 88, 91, 101, 104, 107, 108

Yad Vashem, 94

Yad Vashem Photo Archives, courtesy of United States Holocaust Memorial Museum Photo Archives, 65

About the Author

Bruce L. Brager attended George Washington University in Washington, D.C. He has worked as a staff or freelance writer/editor for many years, specializing in history, political science, foreign policy, and defense/military topics. This is his first book for young adults. He served as an editor for an *American Heritage* CD-ROM on the Civil War, and has published nearly fifty articles for the general market.

Mr. Brager is a native of the Washington, D.C., area and New York City; he lives in Northern Virginia.